# The Poetry of Strangers

# The Poetry of Strangers

What I
Learned
Traveling
America
with a Typewriter

## BRIAN SONIA-WALLACE

HARPER PERENNIAL

NEW YORK • LONDON • TORONTO • SYDNEY • NEW DELHI • AUCKLAND

HARPER ● PERENNIAL

HarperCollins books may be purchased for educational, business, or sales promotional use. For information, please email the Special Markets Department at SPsales@harpercollins.com.

FIRST EDITION

*Designed by Jen Overstreet*

Library of Congress Cataloging-in-Publication Data

Names: Sonia-Wallace, Brian, author.
Title: The poetry of strangers : what I learned traveling America with a typewriter / Brian Sonia-Wallace.
Description: First edition. | New York : Harper Perennial, [2020] | Summary: "Before he became an award-winning writer and poet, Brian Sonia-Wallace set up a typewriter on the street with a sign that said "Poetry Store" and discovered something surprising: all over America, people want poems"— Provided by publisher.
Identifiers: LCCN 2020013534 (print) | LCCN 2020013535 (ebook) | ISBN 9780062870223 (paperback) | ISBN 9780062870247 (ebook)
Subjects: LCSH: Sonia-Wallace, Brian. | Sonia-Wallace, Brian—Travel. | Poets, American—21st century—Biography. | Poetry—Authorship.
Classification: LCC PS3619.O533 Z46 2020 (print) | LCC PS3619.O533 (ebook) | DDC 811/.6—dc23
LC record available at https://lccn.loc.gov/2020013534
LC ebook record available at https://lccn.loc.gov/2020013535

ISBN 978-0-06-287022-3

20 21 22 23 24  LSC  10 9 8 7 6 5 4 3 2 1

*For my mother, who taught me to take care of stories*

*"How do you delete?"*

—every eight-year-old born in the twenty-first century,
using a typewriter for the first time

# Contents

# The Poetry of Strangers

# The First
# Stranger

*When you are grown, no part of you*
*will be recognizable.*
*Will you tend the garden of yourself?*
*Do you dare brave the soil?*

I sat behind a borrowed Smith Corona manual typewriter with sticky keys at a street party in downtown Los Angeles. The year was 2012, and I had recently returned to California from college abroad, another unemployed millennial at the tail end of the financial crisis, looking for a purpose but willing to settle for moving out of his parents' house.

The pounding summer heat at the street party was broken by the shade of skyscrapers, glass citadels to wealth and power that towered over everyone. A new metro line had just been built in this car-powered city, and everyone was celebrating at the grand opening of the latest station. Naturally, to get there, I drove.

Helicopter moms buzzed around their children, *paleteros* called "*hielos!*" and pushed ice cream carts, and a homeless man shouted himself hoarse and broke down on the street corner at all these people in his living room. LA was in the middle of a homelessness crisis, a gentrification crisis, a transportation crisis. LA was perpetually in the midst of these crises.

Next to me a DJ booth, powered by solar panels, played Pharrell Williams's "Happy."

I was nervous, palms sweating as I set out a Costco tray table and folding chair. Another birthday in my sputtering adulthood had passed and I had a leftover length of blue wrapping paper that I made into a sign:

**POETRY STORE**

give me a topic
I'll write you a poem
pay me what you think it's worth

Just a week before, I had heard a story on the radio about someone selling poems in a park, and with an invitation to do *something* at the street party and the yearning only a twenty-two-year-old can have to make a good impression, I thought I might as well give it a try.

*What's the worst that can happen?* I reasoned with my terror. No one stops, and I write poems for myself in public, like a weirdo, and go home. I've been a weirdo before. I can do it again.

I took a picture on my iPhone of the typewriter and reluctantly put it back in my pocket, shoving down the urge to Facebook, to text, to be anywhere but here, on the hot and crowded street corner, surrounded by strangers with an open invitation for any one of them to come up and talk to me.

I idly typed on a piece of paper to calm my nerves. No sooner had I started writing than people drifted over, curious to see the typewriter and then bemused at the prospect of finding a self-proclaimed poet behind it. "Do you need a poem?" I asked them, from under my newsie-style flatcap. I'd done acting and wore this hat like a costume, like armor. I wasn't me, I told myself over and over again, I was the character of the poet. If people rejected me, they weren't rejecting me, they were rejecting this character I was playing.

But people stopped almost immediately. Old folks, to reminisce over the typewriter. Curious kids and their parents. Couples on dates. I asked each of them the same question:

"Do you need a poem?"

"I don't have any money," replied a buzz-cut Chicana woman, with tattoos peeking out wherever clothing met skin.

"That's okay," I replied.

"About my dad, then." Her answer was instant. "He was a long-haul trucker when my brothers and sisters and I were growing up, so he wasn't able to be around much . . ." She drifted into stories of her dad, her family, reminiscing about her life and relationships to a complete stranger on the street while throngs of people passed. "My dad would be gone for weeks at a time, but he'd do it to be able to send money home," she told me. "I would just want him to know that we—that I—understood. And that we loved him for it."

She stopped and stood in silence. I wondered if this story was a weight she'd been carrying for a long time.

My fingers struggled to muster enough force on the rusty keys of the typewriter in front of me to smash the tiny hammers into the ink ribbon and onto paper. I quickly discarded the ten-finger-typing we'd been assured in school was the secret to success and went back to hunt-and-peck.

As I typed each line, the typewriter would skip ever perilously closer to the edge of the cheap TV-tray table, threatening to topple off. I'd have to pause to wrestle it back, turn the knob, pull the carriage back, and start a new line. The c stuck. The spacebar some-times skipped and left two spaces. Any hope I had at formatting the thing was gone—it would format itself, thank you very much.

My index fingers labored over the keyboard. Each keystroke was an exclamation of the permanence.

I didn't keep any pictures of the poems I wrote back then, so I'll never know what the first poem I wrote for a stranger said. I remember images of truck side mirrors, endless lonely roads, buoyed by thoughts of family back home, the road itself becom-ing a vein through which blood flowed back to the heart. And I remember reading the poem to this fierce woman, peeking up to see her eyes closed. It was a first draft, imperfect, riddled with the errors of a sixty-year-old machine and a twenty-two-year-old poet. But it was hers.

At the end, she took a deep breath in, then opened her eyes to look at me. She took her poem, expression inscrutable.

"Wait here," she said, and vanished into the crowd.

I moved on to write for someone new, a middle-aged woman in festive summer clothes who fawned over photos of her dog with me at the typewriter. But then the trucker's daughter reemerged from the mass and pressed a crisp bill into my hand. "I had to go to an ATM," she told me, by way of explanation. Her tone was gruff, but I could see something had softened in her face.

The trucker's daughter didn't look like she had much, but her five dollars was much more than five dollars to an unemployed kid looking for something to hold on to. It was an affirmation, in this world bound by money and scarcity, this world where it's hard to find the words to tell someone how you feel, what you mean. She was sending me a message:

"What you are doing is *worth* something."

Poetry had always seemed like the most impractical of the arts, a throwback as much as the typewriter, the purview now only of English teachers and resentful students. I liked poetry but didn't love it. As a junior nerd I'd proudly memorized poems from the fantasy books I read, and as a young adult had the mandatory Ginsberg *Howl* and Kerouac phase. I never took a poetry class in college but performed lots of student Shakespeare and grudgingly came to like that, for the theater first and the language second. If you had asked me the day before I wrote a poem for the trucker's daughter, "Do you love poetry?" I would have said, "No."

But what I made at the typewriter wasn't what I'd ever thought of as poetry. It was the shrapnel interactions left behind, bits of other people buried in me, leaving me less alone. In a time when social connections were fraying, somehow poetry let me invite people in and empathize with them, whatever story they held. It was poetry that led me to discover a private America, an America where intimacy was possible, one person at a time.

At first, I was convinced it was a scam, that I was pulling a fast one getting people to pay for an index card of blank verse. "That's the dream," a palm reader I became friends with told me conspiratorially. "Roll into town, make your money, and then leave! Dustbowl style." I had a vision of California in the past, orange groves teeming with newly displaced Midwesterners alongside Chinese and Mexican immigrants, workers tilling land that they'd never own. These were families uprooted from the social order and cast adrift to find new places in society. "The harvest gypsies," Steinbeck called them. In the stories, there'd always be the hustler, the swindler, the snake-oil salesman profiting off the hardworking folks. I won't deny there was a certain level of glee in imagining myself in this role.

But the more I wrote poems for strangers in public, the more I came to see a real, deep need that I was fulfilling. All across America, people stop for a poet at a typewriter. It's a cottage industry at this point. Poets' Row in New Orleans is famous, and almost every major metro area supports a few street poets, old and young, with day jobs and without. There are reports of street typewriter poets in the US since at least the 1980s, and in railway stations in Brazil and India, countries with lots of folks who can't read or write, it's still common to find someone at a typewriter helping people get what they need to say down in words. But in the US, where most people can read or write, there's something else afoot: a crisis of emotional and creative illiteracy.

Far from an obsolete art form, I realized poetry could be a solution. The typewriter becomes a line thrown from our digital age back into the past, a way for people to let down the perpetual fixation on appearances and go deeper. When I ask, "What do you need a poem about?" people tell me about their lovers, their devoted partners of many years, their long-distance relationships. They tell me about their dogs and cats. They tell me about their anxiety, their fear, their uncertainty about the future. They tell me about their loss. Their hope. Their dreams.

Companies started hiring my colleagues and me for corporate events, to my amazement and chagrin. After years of writing on the street and at events, out of nearly five thousand applicants, I became the first writer-in-residence at the Mall of America, as well as the poet-in-residence for Amtrak trains and the darling of corporate gigs from Google to investment firms. University fellowships and residencies had little use for me—I had no formal credentials and meager publications. I didn't make any promises of great literature, only that I'd show up and listen well.

Inadvertently, I'd stumbled onto a new model for making art that would change my life: poetry as a service industry.

My writing spaces offered no quiet and I didn't want it. A sensitive city kid like me is used to blocking out too much stimuli, unnerved by silence and lonesomeness. The typewriter let me get back onto my block, into the real world, into community. It let me get offline and start reconnecting, one person at a time. Traveling on the corporate dollar, I got the chance to look at what was poetic in each of the places I visited, how, in each, poetry could unlock the permission people need in their everyday lives to be more honest, connected, fully human selves. How could a mall be a religious experience? A rave a way to cope with grief? Could the best way to make a friend be to ride a train?

"Poetry [is] language that envies a scene it is describing," says critic Wayne Koestenbaum. Envy goes beyond seeing a person. To envy someone is to want to become them. It's no accident, I think, that Koestenbaum is queer like me. There's an understanding of what it's like, from the outside, to look in. In order to write for people, I realize, the idea of "tolerance" falls well short of the mark. I couldn't just refrain from judging my subjects—I had to envy them, to realize how their lives were beautiful in ways mine might never be and speak to that.

My poems use "I" and "you" and "we" interchangeably as pronouns.

In response to the malaise of modern life, we need a paradigm shift in how we think about creativity. Today, we say "someone is a genius," but the ancient Romans would have put it differently. It's not that someone *is* a genius, but that someone *has* a genius. Like the ancient Greeks and their muses, the Romans believed that creativity originated not inside of us, but through our interaction with an external force.

It's tempting to think about creativity as isolated and isolating. Our stories about artists are full of lone tortured geniuses: Van Gogh cutting off his ear, or Emily Dickinson alone for years in her room. The untold stories in this book offer a counterpoint. They show how creativity can unfold between people, as the glue that binds communities together in divisive times. Creativity is finding two unlike things and saying, "You know what, these two aren't so different after all." Each time we find ourselves in each other, despite each other, despite all our differences, that is the most incredible act of creativity.

Connection across difference is at the heart of poetry—we call it a metaphor, a comparison without "like" or "as."

"This is like therapy!" people tell me constantly at the typewriter, surprised by their own response to the simple, absurd question, "What do you need a poem about?" Across America, people become open books, dissolve into tears, even offer up legal tender when an anonymous stranger at a typewriter offers to write them a poem.

Everyone thinks Americans don't want to talk to each other.

In reality, we're all just dying to be heard.

# Becoming the Typewriter

The last old-school typewriter factory in the world closed the year before I touched my first typewriter. It shuttered its doors forever in Mumbai in 2011. But these machines, made before manufacturers started building in planned obsolescence, have outlasted the companies that made them. Typewriters were postwar machines, first mass-manufactured in the United States at rifle factories with names like Remington after the Civil War to keep the assembly lines humming as the demand for weapons went down. The story of the typewriter is a footnote in the mad dash for mechanization and efficiency that led to its demise. But the stampede of progress left weird holdovers and niche communities in its wake, collectors' groups and repair enthusiasts, drawn to the writing machine's storied past.

The original inventors of the machine would have no use for it now. They were after efficiency, and in the modern day I imagine they'd be app designers. But what they built endures. The typewriter is better, at least in my line of work, *because* it's harder and slower. On a typewriter, it feels less like you are writing and more like you are composing. It's an emotional machine, one that bears the imprints of its use. The typewriter becomes a retreat, an escape from the social, the online, the world of meme where you can print things out in endless repetition and variation. On the typewriter, the world is fixed—you know where you are.

A poet is like a typewriter, in many ways. A poet is a train in a world of cars. A thing that has died and is still holding on. The poet is the thing for the few, the stragglers, the maladaptors and survivors. Every year, someone declares poetry dead. Every year, people write poetry. To be a poet is to recognize that obsolescence can be beautiful, that change does not always reduce, but rather reinvents.

Like the typewriter, I didn't start by writing my own stories, I was just a vehicle people used to say what they needed to say through my poetry. I later learned that, like the word *computer*, typewriter originally referred not just to the machine, but to the person using the machine.

I didn't know it when I started, but I wasn't just writing *on* the typewriter.

I was *becoming* the typewriter.

Here's how it began. In September 2014, I accidentally started a poetry business with a $20 garage sale typewriter and an impending sense of doom. It was meant to be a one-month performance-art experiment, somewhere between an avant-garde solo show and a practical joke. "I'm going to pay my rent with poetry!" I said, giddy with the absurdity of it and despair about everything else. It felt like my life was over, so why not do something stupid.

"I have zero income for next month," I confided in a friend.

"The candle store where I work always needs people around the holidays," he offered helpfully. "It's minimum wage retail."

I'll confess to being prideful and privileged. I had a degree, had been working toward white-collar success. "Downwardly mobile," the newspapers were saying about my generation, and I was terrified of that. So many of us were leaving college jobless and indebted, tucking our dreams into our back pockets. In the twenty-first century's freelance, on-demand world, each of us was our own business, offering service to the highest bidder. Gone were the days of lifelong company employment—my recession-graduate friends were Lyft drivers and Airbnb hosts. *Could the same thing work for artists?* I wondered. Doing freelance fundraising for the occasional arts nonprofit, the same nagging thought had always tickled the back of my mind. *Why are you raising money to help other people make their art, to build their dream? Why not build your own?*

I'd done poetry on the street a few times since my first brush with it, and always got good tips, so I figured it might not be *impossible.*

It was a path I would never have seen coming. My interest in literature and desire to make any time to read or write waned in my early twenties when I moved back to LA after college and into adulthood. I had grown up in LA, but a child's city is very different from an adult's realities. I imagined pursuing an artistic career, living in a kind of happy poverty, but found myself stuck in a cycle of unpaid internships and days I couldn't get out of bed, trolling Craigslist wanted ads instead of reading great minds.

When I found a job, I took it gladly, putting my skills to use by writing grants for a community development nonprofit. Among other things, my work focused on finding funding to fight for a pathway to legitimacy for the street vendors who sold tacos and bacon-wrapped hot dogs from carts around LA County, scrappy entrepreneurs who turned nothing into something with hard work and the magic of the streets. I would still go to arts events in the evenings or take the typewriter out when I could, on the weekends. It was a cute thing I did on the side, a few times a year. I started meeting other poets and typewriter enthusiasts, who became "non-work friends."

Work took a turn for the unexpected when I left one job only to be laid off from another within six months. I spent the following six months polishing my résumé, putting on suits, and driving to interviews once—twice—three times, always to end up as a "second choice" candidate behind someone else with more experience.

To top it all off, I had just broken up with my first long-term boyfriend, the one I was with when I came out to my parents. When we broke up, I came home to find a homemade book of poems on top of a pile of my things that he was returning. It was the book I'd made of love poems I'd written about him since we got together, a one-year anniversary gift.

Crying, I ripped the book to shreds.

My ex had just started a job as a corporate attorney, and the apartment we moved into was at the top of my price range. Every month unemployed and interviewing, I beat the pavement for freelance work and spent down my savings just to cover my portion of rent for the apartment I no longer wanted to live in. As winter set in, the freelance work dried up.

When my parents offered to take me with them to visit my grandparents in Missouri, I jumped at the chance to get away from everything. They bought the plane ticket. My ex was traveling too, sending a constant stream of Airbnb guests to pay his portion of the rent and remind me of his absence. He ran to Peru. I ran to Missouri.

My grandparents live in Columbia, a college town where they both taught at the university. When we visit, my mom fills the freezer with enough homemade food to last them a lifetime, never mind that my grandfather, a first-generation Polish Jew, is perfectly happy with his Sam's Club cold cuts. The pace of life is slower there. People pop in and out of the house, dinners sprawl into evenings, and even my grandfather's need to be constantly busy is satisfied just by walking the dog most of the time. The basement, where the guest rooms are, is drafty in autumn, the linoleum floor cold and relatively bare compared to the clutter of upstairs. Here, at last, away from it all, I had time and space to think.

Amanda Palmer's TED Talk, "The Art of Asking," had recently come out, and I listened to it on a loop. In it, she describes going from working as a living statue to running the first million-dollar crowdfunding campaign for an album in an age when record labels were going bankrupt because everyone was pirating songs. "Don't make people pay for music," Palmer intones. "*Ask* them to." The image of the trucker's daughter went around and around in my head, the way her face looked when I read her poem, how I felt when she came back with money after I'd given her something for free.

So, with my personal and professional life in shambles, I sketched out how many days a month I thought I'd need to write for tips to make my rent.

It was all of them.

I knew I had to hold myself accountable if I wanted to make sure I actually followed through and didn't fall into laziness and despair. I'd run Kickstarter campaigns before, and this would be just like that, I thought. Rule #1 of the twenty-first century: It's not real unless it's online. The blessing of social media was that practically everyone I'd ever met in adulthood was still connected to me, and I knew that even if none of them read my posts, the sheer act of posting for everyone would give me the peer pressure I'd need to follow through. So I fired up my laptop and hit *record*.

"I'm going to try to pay my rent with poetry," I told no one, from my grandparents' cold and empty basement in Missouri. I had no higher aspirations. This was just about survival.

Back in LA, I set my typewriter up anywhere I thought there might be a crowd, every night, for a month. Everywhere from sidewalks outside art gallery openings to swap meets and food truck festivals. Anywhere people would have time and loose change. No venue would hire me to perform poems, I was a nobody. But I was a nobody with a typewriter, and I had access to the street.

The word *busk* comes from the old French word *busquer*, meaning to seek. Originally it was a nautical term, used to talk about ships tacking to and fro to find the wind. It was only in the mid-nineteenth century that the word gained its present meaning: to go around performing, for tips. The term *busking* usually refers to musicians who set up instruments on the street corner, play, and solicit donations. The first evening of my absurd challenge, I packed my car with a Costco tray table, folding chair, and my Lettera 32 teal typewriter. I drove to Hollywood. Where dreams come true?

I knew of a running spoken word night called Da Poetry Lounge that always had a crowd out the door an hour before it started. Ignoring the sign-up list for poets wanting to perform onstage, I set my typewriter up right next to the line to write for one person at a time, moving a few feet every ten minutes for a new customer. A young black woman dressed to the nines came up to me first—she didn't know that I wasn't affiliated with the show, didn't know the challenge I'd set for myself, I was just part of her wild Tuesday night out. And she wanted a poem.

"About butterflies!" she told me. But then she included me in her conversation with her friends about how she was coming up on a breakup anniversary with her first serious boyfriend, a

man she had entered adulthood with but was now absent. I felt
a pang for my ex. Halfway through the poem, my ribbon ran to
the end, and I had to remove the spools to wind them back, my
fingers turning black in the process. When I pulled the finished
poem from the machine, they left a black smudge on the corner, a
fingerprint signature.

"Can I read you your poem?" I asked my new patron. It
seemed like an intimate thing, a reading—like something that
needed consent. She nodded, and there in the line of young hopeful poets desperate to be seen, I read in a quiet voice, just to her:

For Monique,

> Flap those wings
> wet from the chrysalis
> believe you can fly
> at least flutter
> the flame is burning
> burning low
> that blue, almost out
> kinda flame.
> Cup it in your palms
> don't let it die—
> on our anniversary, he gave me
> 20 red roses
> and I think I cried,
> I don't remember.

It happened so long ago
        and I was still a caterpillar,
        a blue flame.
Not 20, not yet
        just a single rose.

Reading back now, I'm struck that what I wrote uses just about every poetry metaphor cliché in the book. Butterflies and roses and fires, oh my! But after I finished reading, the woman just hugged me for a long time. Person after person in line got a poem, and I told them, "Pay me what you think it's worth," and they paid me more than nothing. The more-than-nothings added up.

Pumped up on my success in line, I signed up for three minutes onstage. I told the assembled crowd my goal, my challenge, my practical joke: "This month, I'm going to pay my rent with poetry!" The sweaty room of poets laughed. Everyone was in on the impossible joke. There were professional poets here, spoken word artists who performed for a living and came here to hone their craft—but they worked their way up in spaces like this for years, some decades, and only a tiny percentage ever were able to make careers of it. When I sat down, the host got up with one raised eyebrow and said, "If you figure out how to pay rent writing poems, tell me how! I've been trying to do that for years."

At an ArtWalk in Frogtown, a little boy danced up to me with his worn-out mother. Laughing manically, the boy insisted I write a poem about "crazy chicken!" and I diligently set to work:

For Carlo,

with the squawking, leg-
  tied, going crazy
    pollo loco
energy, madness
 TAG YOU'RE IT
    laughing tumbling
  exhausted out of
    breath
panting, hands on knees
  chicken-dancing home
  to collapse
like so many drumsticks
    into bed
   into fried dreams
   knobby-elbowed night
  pecking at the
  tiny pinpricks
  of reality
    scattered through
  this chicken-scratch
  illegible life

A few days later, I got an email from the boy's mother, who'd
tracked me down online. It turned out she was an attorney and

wanted to know if I could come write poetry for a fundraiser she was hosting.

Unknowingly, I'd just secured my first paid corporate gig. It wouldn't be the last.


At a taco truck street festival a few blocks from Venice Beach, the night was wild and shrouded in mist. It was the perfect context for busking—young people a few drinks in who came with cash in hand for tacos but, once they finished eating, started roaming the streets looking for something more to do. A few musicians had figured this out and set up every few blocks with guitars, but I was the only typewriter.

I'd been writing for a few hours when a bear of a man exploded from the mist, boisterously drunk. His jaw dropped when he saw the typewriter. "What are you *doing*?" he shouted with open arms and a pumpkin grin that split his face in two.

I explained my project to him, and his excitement verged on obscene. "Let's get you your rent!" he shouted. "I work for a big real estate company, lots of money. Here, let me give you my number . . ."

He didn't have a card, so I slid over and offered him the typewriter. He spelled out his phone number in letters—t-h-r-e-e o-n-e z-e-r-o—he was too drunk to realize that the typewriter had number keys.

I called the next day, uncertain if he'd even remember me, but with no job and no other prospects, my boldness got the better of my fear.

"Hi, Jonathon, I'm Brian . . . the poet . . . you left your phone number on my typewriter . . ."

Next thing I knew, I was setting up my typewriter next to the bar at a real estate company's bocce ball tournament, being offered cocktails by HR.

On the street, only the truly curious would approach me. At corporate events these patrons were joined by the bored and ine-briated. "Write me a poem about my ass!" a drunk woman in a little sundress at my first corporate event slurred, spurred on by her friends. When I read them the ode, the homage, com-plete with Nicki Minaj references, they laughed and the woman's friends high-fived her. I laughed with them. I guess sometimes what's needed is not deep processing but celebration.

*Your body is a novel*—that poem ends—*well, I'm a voracious reader.*

Jonathon was just the first, and drunkest, person to see the po-tential for what I was doing with poetry in corporate America. By the end of the night when I met him at the beach, I had a card from an investment banker who was organizing a conference af-terparty at the Hilton, and an offer to do a weekly haiku column for Dollar Shave Club's lifestyle blog.

Appearing in corporate spaces with my flatcap and typewriter I was aware of eyes on me. But I was used to being the weirdo, the outsider. Part of me liked the way people's eyebrows raised when I said, "This is my job" in response to the perpetual ques-tion: "What do you *really* do?" I felt a mix of pity for this promising young kid stuck in the dead-end service industry event world without dreams of climbing higher, and envy at the idea of going all in to be a writer. I would eat with the servers, but the people I wrote poems for would bring me glasses of wine from the bar, an odd sense of reciprocity in the exchanging of gifts.

John Green, the young adult author, describes all writing as making a gift: "Like a good gift, you can't worry too much about people saying 'I love it!'—you just have to worry about making it the best, most thoughtful gift you can make for that person." And, somehow, holding someone's image in mind while I wrote on the street made the writing come clean and fast. In my room, a poem could take hours just figuring out what I wanted to say. On the street, it didn't matter what I wanted to say, I had my instructions and all I had to do was execute them. My goal wasn't literary perfection, it was to move the one person standing in front of me.

I wasn't my target audience, I realized.

Sometimes when I was busking on the street no one stopped, and I made nothing. Sometimes I struck gold. I wrote about whatever the person standing in front of me said, and I'll be the first to confess that I didn't love all the poetry that I wrote. But I never had a person return a poem I'd written for them.

More than writing, what I was giving my patrons was the gift of listening. But I was the beneficiary of vicarious living too, walking a mile in the shoes of anyone who would let me, bearing witness to their struggles and triumphs.

It made me realize that traditional creative spaces can be counterproductive precisely because they are divorced from the audiences who will finally see what gets made there. Of course there's a huge value to incubation time, but so often what I would create in private wasn't that interesting to anyone else. I was writing what *I* needed, but not necessarily what was needed in the world. In theater, where I started, it was so easy to spend hours in rehearsals behind closed doors and then wonder why audiences didn't come.

In contrast, people would stop whatever they were doing to come to the typewriter. They'd look uncomfortable for a few seconds when I asked what they needed a poem about, then open up completely. Something about the presence of an anachronism-laden poet demanded it, whatever the context. I knew few of my patrons had read even a single poem since high school. But they were reverent when I handed them the scraps of paper on which I recorded and transformed the stories they shared with me into something resembling a poem. The concept of "poetry" itself was romantic, even nostalgic, much like the typewriter, the byproduct of a bygone era with all the allure of the past, but living and breathing and right in front of them, something they could talk to, a legacy to find themselves in or else insert themselves and correct the record.

What jailbreaking the writer's desk from the study did was invite real-time collaboration and exchange, not just with people who considered themselves artists but with folks from all walks of life. Often, as I wrote, people would keep talking, unable to stop sharing details of their lives. Writing became a game, a mad dash to translate new information into metaphor and verse in real time.

Not content just to receive poems, some people at the type-writer would share poems they'd written with me, often pieces of writing they'd never showed anyone but carried privately for years. They weren't asking for feedback, just for me to see what they'd done, like they were trying to find out, not if the poems were good, but if something as intimate as someone's first attempts at poetry was even *allowed*.

What I didn't expect was that my relationship with Jonathon from the real estate company would continue for years—that he'd eventually invite me to his wedding, that I'd hold his firstborn child and write a poem for her years later. My poems hang on that family's walls. "I was just out of a bad breakup," Jonathon says, recounting the story of how we met years later, "I was looking for something to hang on to. Then you appeared out of the mist!" This is the story that he tells people when they ask how he got interested in art and started writing poetry—and now he's pro-lific, and not shy about it, performing his own writing all over LA.

I was taking a break from writing at an ArtWalk when I offered my spot at the typewriter to an eight-year-old girl. I was ahead of my goal, halfway through the month challenge to pay rent with poetry. I had been writing in the sun for hours on the riverfront as families passed by on their way between galleries and kids' activities. The girl at my typewriter was the child of the street ven-dors selling food under a tent next to me and had been watching me work silently for the last ten minutes. Whenever kids came to my typewriter, I'd learned to let them have a turn rather than trying to write for them. This was partly generosity and partly self-preservation—kids could be the harshest critics.

The quiet girl sat down at the typewriter, tentative at first as she learned her way around the machine. Most kids write their names and are content to do that and then wander off, but not her. I waited a few minutes, watching her write with complete concentration and no signs of slowing down. It was the perfect time to take a break and get a burrito. When I turned back, the child had a line of people waiting to get a poem from her!

What I was selling was not even poetry, it was the presence of the poet: a performance of listening and writing. Anyone could do that performance, and so the poet could be anyone—in fact, the little girl totally upstaged me. In her first half hour as a poet, she made eight dollars and got an invitation from the festival organizers to write at an event they were hosting the next week. Could they borrow my typewriter?

As the girl wrote, her mother, who was selling tacos next door, came over to make sure everything was okay and watched her daughter entrance a crowd of strangers with only her words. As the child finished each poem, she'd sign it, like a rock star selling T-shirts, and calmly hand it to the person in front of her. Then she'd turn to load the typewriter for the next person, the next poem, as she'd seen me do, as she'd seen her mother do a hundred times before with tortillas instead of paper.

I developed a little rubric for myself, four elements that I saw crop up again and again in poems that got the best reactions from people. I started to check these off in my poems as I wrote: something beautiful, something surprising, something familiar—and a joke, so that the work didn't take itself too seriously.

Writing in public got me thinking about ideal working conditions for creativity differently. British philosopher Alain de Botton talks about the terror of a writing desk, the quiet way that offices and studies can make the fear of failure overwhelming. In his book *A Week at the Airport*, he lives in London Heathrow Airport's Terminal 5 as their writer-in-residence. "Original thoughts are like shy animals," he says from his desk in front of Departures. "We sometimes have to look the other way—towards a busy street or terminal—before they run out of their burrows."

Like de Botton, I found the messiness of writing out in public, the overstimulation, took away my fear. Even the typewriter contributed, clacking and sticking midword with stubborn keys. My internal critic couldn't get a word in edgewise over all the noise! And because people were literally watching me write their poems, I gave up on writing the "best poem." I just didn't have time. If people were emotional, it was because their stories were emotional. If they were invested in what they told me, they'd be invested in the poem. I was incidental to the experience—an unknown guy on the street just helping get down raw emotion and messy stories in words.

I called my monthlong challenge "RENT Poet," which doubled as a statement of my goal (to pay rent) and also as a play on words with the phrase "rent boy," which I thought was a widely understood term for a male prostitute—someone who sells intimacy for cash. Apparently the term isn't well known outside of the UK and the gay community in the US, though, and everyone I talked to, from soccer moms to CEOs, heard it as "Rent-a-Poet." They thought it was so, *so* cute.

Ironically, in my month of busking I ended up making California minimum wage entirely with the money people paid for their poems, earning the same amount that I would have working forty-hour weeks in retail at the candle store. I had paid my rent and then some, but it didn't stop there. The first corporate gigs turned into an ongoing stream of referrals for never-ending weddings and holiday parties, and I banded together with some friends who'd formed the Melrose Poetry Bureau.

By going straight to the street for my public, suddenly I found a wealth of people interested in poetry who were not plugged into the traditional networks. It was as simple as getting out of the car, as sharing space. I found my poetry lovers at taco trucks, not at literary mixers. In fact, I had bypassed the traditional gatekeepers of the literary world completely and was paying my rent with my poetry within a month. It was inconstant work, riddled with worry about money, but it was happening.

It seems like no coincidence that same year I tried my initial RENT Poet experiment, poet Rupi Kaur blew up on Instagram and self-published her debut book, *milk and honey*, which outsold the year's Pulitzer Prize winner by a factor of ten. She'd bypassed publishing to find her own readers, and they responded. Suddenly, poetry was on the bestseller list for the first time in a long time. There was something in the air—people were hungry for it.

If Rupi Kaur was pop-poet royalty, I was essentially a poetry busboy. I wasn't going to rule anything, but I could eke out a living serving people words, one by one. Rather than a million-strong Instagram following, I had a typewriter. But the typewriter was a siren song, the clack of keys making older folks nostalgic and younger ones curious. Someone sitting at a laptop or with a notepad wants to be left alone. Someone sitting at a typewriter wants you to talk to them.

I developed a standard line for the retirees who liked to stop to sarcastically ask me, the millennial, "What *is* that?"

"Oh this?" I'd say. "You haven't seen it? It's the new iPad!"

# Railroad Writer

> *"The fire-alarm bells in this city [St. Louis] were struck at six minutes to 2 o'clock this afternoon, in responses to the blows of the hammer which drove the last spike in the Union Pacific Railroad. Quite a crowd assembled at the telegraph office, and much interest was manifest on the occasion. Everybody is rejoiced at the completion of the grandest enterprise ever accomplished by mortal hands!"*

> —*The Highland Weekly News*, Hillsborough, Ohio, May 20, 1869

In 2016, I win one of the coveted writer's residencies on Amtrak, a carte blanche ticket to go anywhere I want on the train, expenses paid, and write. I'm ecstatic—then paralyzed.

I realize I have nowhere to go. A residency like this calls for an epic cross-country trip, a buddy movie in the making, but it's a ticket for one. I'm a writer who thrives on connection, a theater geek turned poet, an only child whose only fear is being left alone with his own thoughts. The prospect of being trapped in a rapidly moving metal box to marinate my demons seemed romantic when I wrote the proposal, but I've happily woken up now.

A year passes.

I'm running up against the statute of limitations for this trip, use it or lose it. Under the wire, I get a second residency—this one at the Mall of America in Minnesota—and then an invitation comes in to do poetry at a music festival in Michigan. I set my sights, book my tickets, and pack my bags. In total, I'll be traveling across the country for over a month, with ten days all told sealed into the train watching the mesas of New Mexico turn into the post-industrial northern half of the Midwest, and back again. The train is Manifest Destiny, "go west, young man," but I'm starting in LA so I'll have to go east, backward in time, cutting against the grain of history.

While an elderly woman with heaps of bags screams down the vastness of the station for a conductor to help her, a wizened man passes me boarding the train. He sways dangerously up the stairs, ignoring my offer to help as if he couldn't hear it. But when I get to the upper deck, I find him sitting on the bed in *my* box-size room. I realize I'd left the door open.

"This your room?" he wheezes.

"Yeah."

"I think I'm across the hall." There's a sheepish pause. "How do you open the doors?"

Having used his last energy to tackle the stairs, the old guy finally found himself defeated by a sliding door.

My new neighbor's name, I learn, is Oren, and it is the first time either of us has been on an Amtrak train.

We leave at dusk. LA is lit up, orange hills and concrete rivers.

We pass through fields of rubble, pallets, and industrial cargo containers, all the machinery of civilization that we keep on the periphery. The train cuts its way through the junkyard of America. The tracks are hidden like a specter from the places people live. On the other side of the industrial wasteland are lonely suburbs, detached houses with grass lawns that look like they've been airlifted to California, leading up to Fullerton Station, a gorgeous mock-Mexican stucco building.

The "roomette," which the Amtrak side advertised as "like a hotel," could just as easily have been advertised as "like a closet" by a less romantic copywriter. The plastic walls touch each end of my narrow bed, and the window over the bed looking outside is barely an arm's length from Oren's archnemesis the door. "Sleeps two," the Amtrak website optimistically proclaimed—and indeed, as I explore the room, I find a handle above the window. I pull it down a thin shelf, directly above my tiny mattress, and discover a pillow and sheets on top of it, which have been wedged against the wall. This is the room's second bed.

Having set my bag down at the foot of the bed, I slide the door open again to go to explore the train. It's divided into sections, a segmented insect, a few cars of roomettes identical to mine (and maybe half-full) leading into a car or two with fewer, slightly larger rooms. The dining car is next, with plastic tables and ornate drapery, and then the observation deck, where windows march up the walls to give views of the outside to passengers sat in blue leather chairs. Beyond the observation deck, I peek into general seating, where I find rows of passengers with airplane pillows settled into recliners that look spacious compared to airplane seats until I remember that these folks have chosen to make this three-day trip without the privilege of lying down for seventy plus hours.

Everything on the train takes place on the second story, whizzing along above the countryside. The first story is just for boarding, baggage, and showers, cut off from onboard life by tight staircases with sharp turns.

On the train's second story, life settles into a routine. Meals are at set times, so my roomette neighbor Oren and I wind our way to the dining car dinner, listing side to side down shoulder-width hallways. Meal times are staggered with the other passengers, but the dining car is never full. It looks like something out of the 1950s, a glorious retro feel mirrored in the staff's uniforms and, more ominously, the racial divide between crew and passengers, at least those coming from the luxury-priced sleeper cars. Each dining car table seats four, and despite the empty tables around us, they pack everyone in elbow to elbow with strangers.

For my first train dinner I splurge and do the surf and turf, valued at thirty dollars on the menu—but hey, it's included with the room, complimentary for the poet on board! I am mad with the power of words to procure steak and shrimp. I eat it for dinner every evening for the next three days.

Oren and I sit next to each other. Despite his massive hearing aids, the ninety-five-year-old catches perhaps one in five words directed his way, so communication with him always feels a bit like talking over old-time ham radio, unsure if the person on this frequency can hear over the static. For this first dinner, we are joined by a round and jolly programmer in his sixties and a lean Boeing engineer in his fifties, who meticulously pronounces his *T*'s. Oren, I learn, was a physician before his retirement, a lifetime ago now—certainly longer than I've been alive. Together, our lives span seventy years of unshared history, and even the engineer and programmer miss each other's references. We laugh anyway.

Without a common past to glory in, we talk systems—airplane black boxes, biologists' failings as coders. When I share my status as the poet on board, they immediately turn to brainstorming productivity: How can I optimize conditions for maximum poetry? Oren beams through the conversation, participating intermittently but mostly holding court, happy to just sit with these precocious youngsters. Through all the chat about train travel and timetables and work, I listen for hints to my dinner companions' emotional lives and families during the conversation. There's talk of a wife here, a vacation there, but mostly we stick to fluid mechanics and aviation principles and how tech jobs have changed since the 1990s. These men all have private lives, I'm sure, but maybe that's just not train talk.

I'm reminded of the intellectual curiosity and stoicism of my dad, somewhere between the programmer and the engineer in age, a lifetime career academic who lives in statistics and big data and has little time for emotions. I know that, as a teenager in the 1960s, my dad collected and sold model trains out of his garage in Missouri—a niche interest in a technology that was already on its way to obsolescence. When he was in high school, my dad was part of the local steam train society with a motley collection of older rail enthusiasts. They would go on trips with a newfangled video camera to see particularly rare antique engines pulling trains to nowhere so rail fans could get an action shot.

I was fascinated by trains as a kid, and around the corner from my house was a big model train store. By the time I entered my teenage years, shortly after 9/11, the train store had moved to a smaller location, which suspiciously caught fire and was rebuilt as a hot tub emporium. I had abandoned my wooden trains and Legos and video games for the theater, decided the terror and eccentricities of other people in the flesh trumped the worlds I could build alone in my room, my only-child room with its loft bed that simulated a bunk bed without a sibling sleeping underneath me.

On my sixteenth birthday, when I was the age my dad started his model train business, he got down a dusty box from the garage and wrapped it for me to open. Inside were tiny, intricate metal trains emblazoned with the logo of a fictional rail company he'd invented himself as a teenager and saved lovingly all these years. In was an inheritance wrapped in tissue paper and carted across the country through thirty years of moves. But I'd outgrown trains by then.

I handled each dusty train carefully, listened to his story about what these scale models had meant. But that was his world, his adolescence, not mine. If he felt disappointment, my father never expressed it. The box of tiny trains sat, untouched, for a few months, before we gave it away.

It makes me think of giving poems away to people, hoping that they will be meaningful in their lives, but also surrendering control of the work as soon as it's out of my hands. You can't control someone's response to a gift. You just have to give and mean it.

Thursday, day two on the train, breaks over the cliffs and mesas of New Mexico, sun staining the desert gold. The train lists and creaks back and forth the same day and night, a refuge for retirees with time for days of travel. There's a remarkable sense of trust here. You leave your room unlocked, your big bags downstairs by the doors. Anyone could conceivably grab them at any stop, but, invariably, they're fine. I eat breakfast with a woman who has a room near the dining car and says, "Hi, sweetie!" as I pass for the rest of the trip. After breakfast, I head to the observation deck with its high glass windows, passing a group of older people huddled in conversation. One of them is saying, "I know it's racist, but . . ." He lowers his voice so I miss the rest.

We're over the rainbow now.

Cell service is patchy in the hours between stops, returning intermittently as we wind through the canyons so that my attempts at phone conversations turn into games of tag. The sleeper car nearest the diner advertises a Wi-Fi password, but even standing in that car my phone can't pick up the signal. It's like the train is forcing its passengers together, willing them to interact.

Over lunch, the retired man opposite me is in a shirt that says "Value Diversity," with pictures of different types of rifles. He brags to me that he's ridden every line both ways, 165,000 miles in total. It's his retirement hobby. I imagine the train as a luxury land-cruiser, now faded, a final diner on the American frontier where it's okay to sit with strangers when the world outside is more parking lots than people.

Oren and I settle into the observation car after each meal, watching the stucco missions go by. I get increasingly restless. I want to write, to uphold my end of the bargain with Amtrak and type poems for passengers, but somehow bringing a typewriter here seems like a transgression. The train may not be the best way to travel anymore, but it does seem to connect people by slowing them down. When everyone is stuck in a box together, the "stop and see!" draw of the typewriter, so powerful in urban settings, is somewhat lessened. I'm trapped in that midpoint between per-mission and subterfuge, a writer-in-residence traveling incognito, with no signage or announcements to let people know I'm sanctioned to be here by Amtrak. Sitting in front of me, at the four-person table across from Oren, my Olivetti 32 feels like a warning rather than an invitation.

Interminable time passes with nothing but sidelong glances from other passengers. Before the railroad, church clock towers struck the hour based on a noon when the sun was directly overhead, so all time was local. The train companies were the ones who pushed for a universal time, set off a standard maritime clock which before had been essential only for sailors charting course. On November 18, 1883, telegraph lines transmitted time signals to all major cities in the US at noon on the dot, wiping out over three hundred local time zones.

As we pass Albuquerque, a middle-aged married couple and the wife's mother get on and strike up a conversation about the typewriter I've had in front of me for nearly an hour. We do the typical train small talk: Where did you get on? Where are you going? Why the train? Jo Ann, the wife, answers instantly. "I don't fly!" It's a common refrain.

Jo Ann and her family are visiting kids and grandkids and are celebrating with Bud Lights at 11:30 A.M. Once we've broken the ice and they've expressed openness to me writing a poem to commemorate the trip, I ask Jo Ann, "What do you need a poem about?" Her response is as instantaneous as it is dreaded.

"Sadie!" she quips.

"Who's Sadie?"

"My dog."

In my experience as a poet for hire, what unites us across the entire US, red and blue, is our urgent need for a poem about our dog. I swallow my snobbery and start to write. I'm halfway through my next poem when Jo Ann's mother interrupts—"I didn't tell you about my dog! I call her Miss Daisy, and I drive her!" A pause for laughter.

But then the woman gets more thoughtful. "I speak to

Miss Daisy in Spanish," the woman tells me, "I don't speak in Spanish much anymore, but I do it for her, for whatever reason." The language of childhood, youth, family. I suddenly have a glimpse of this woman's life in an air-conditioned desert bubble, older and not getting out much, with a little dog as a tether to her humanity.

As I'm writing, a young woman who's been sitting behind me slips me a piece of paper with her topic on it. "I'm Dori, I'm a writer too. Maybe I can write you one . . ." I grin. Finally, the car has transformed into a pop-up poetry salon, passengers at different tables reading and writing. Two little girls with their grandmother pass and type their names on the typewriter. I overhear, from a few tables away, Grandma saying, "Let's play 'make a poem,'" as they sit down. The game lasts just a few minutes given their attention spans before they turn to something else.

"Art is what we take care of," a librarian I sit with at lunch tells me.

Oren sits next to me, at my typewriter, reading paperback Civil War fiction in waking moments between his frequent naps. I finish a poem for a family and have a temporary lull. I look up from the typewriter to find Oren awake, gazing out the window.

"How are you doing?" I ask. He doesn't hear me.

I tap the elder on the shoulder and ask again, shouting in his face to be heard. "When was the last time you were on a train?" I ask, making small talk.

"It was in 1943," Oren tells me, "coming back from the army." I learn that Oren is headed from California, where he lives now, to visit his older brother in his hometown in Indiana. "My brother is ninety-six, a year older than me," Oren tells me, a note of smugness creeping into his voice. "He has a caregiver!"

Oren's last time on a train was when he moved to California with his wife after being discharged from the service with a disability, unable to serve on the European front of World War II. It's only now that we've been sitting together and sharing meals for days that Oren finally opens up to me about his marriage, beaming that his wife was his better half. She was half Native American, he tells me, and people in their small town were so horrible to her that she had to leave, dropping out of high school and seeking a new, better life. When the couple moved to California, she hid her ancestry. It was a fresh start for them both.

They lived and worked in California for forty years, until, on retirement, they bought an RV. As we ride the train tracks between LA and Chicago, Oren reminisces to me about the places he visited with his wife in that RV. In New Mexico, he points out that we are passing by Trinity, the site the US tested its first nuclear bomb—the bomb that ended the war for Oren's generation. It's open to tourists only once a year.

Oren tells me about visiting the site, twenty years ago now, making the pilgrimage to where it all ended, or it all began. His wife declined to join him and stayed in the RV. "She wasn't interested in all that."

It was only three years ago she died. He can't talk about her long without a tear coming into his eye.

"You're my minder!" Oren tells me as we make our way back to our rooms. He won't let me help him down the lurching corridor of the train, but he concedes to let me carry his book so he can use both hands to steady himself on the walls.

I haven't worked up the courage to write Oren a poem yet. He would never ask. But I know I want to.

Over meals, train old-timers fill me in on the various Amtrak routes they've ridden, and I leaf through a brochure getting a sense of the intricacies of the sprawling system. The train from Chicago to Minneapolis, which ends at Seattle, is called the Empire Builder, a Manifest Destiny throwback. It seems to me that we aren't so sure about "empire" as an objective anymore. The service from LA to Chicago, which Oren and I are riding together, is called the Southwest Chief, one racial epithet away from "Redskins." Maybe if someone was making billions from it, activists would be up in arms to change the name—but, like the train itself, it remains an artifact of history, not quite buried in the sand.

In 1997, Congress asked Amtrak to find a way to operational self-sufficiency, making enough to run the trains without a direct subsidy. In 2002, the company's new president, just over a month into his tenure, told Congress that "Amtrak will never be profitable." The issue is the infrastructure—even though train ridership is up, the company is already so far behind on essen-

tial maintenance for equipment from years of insufficient budgets
that it would take an ungodly infusion of cash to save the whole
operation from its slow descent into rust.

The train starts to fill up as we get into the Midwest, the flat
expanse of Kansas that seems to go on forever. Desert gives way
to farmland, and around Topeka the train starts to get busy with
day-trippers and short-haul commuters. I've never seen the Amish
before but recognize them instantly as we chug our way toward
Kansas City, ruddy-faced in plain woven clothes, beards and bonnets, chatting gaily in their neo-Germanic language as we pass
through miles of farmland. I notice one of the men looking intently at my typewriter and I ask if he needs a poem.

He and his three table companions are moving to Kansas,
he tells me in quiet but confident English, and are heading back
from buying the property to get their belongings. When I ask him
what he needs a poem about, he pauses, then says, "Hoping to be
good neighbors." He talks about the local community where they
are headed, how much they know it's hurting economically, and
their hope that their contribution can help. It flies in the face of
the isolationist, detached stereotype of the Amish that I have. I
imagine the local people not understanding them, fearing them,
talking shit behind their backs.

I write Robert Frost's line, "Good fences make good neighbors."

In Frost's poem "Mending Wall," the elements are always

eating away at a stone wall, which the property owner on the other side insists they rebuild each year, a collaborative exercise in exclusion. Frost's narrator is not a fan but does not refuse to participate.

I write the Amish family, "We leave the wall down."

It's only months later that I learn that the first transcontinental railroad in the US, linking California to the East Coast, was one of the crowning achievements of Abraham Lincoln. In the era of the Civil War, it was a symbolic binding together of the divided country.

Amtrak is still freedom, albeit for different people—for the old and those afraid to fly, for people society has left behind in its inexorable march of progress and for those who themselves have rejected society. The ridership are retirees and libertarians and antique collectors, engine enthusiasts and conspiracy theorists and people who live off the grid and work the land. The people I encounter on Amtrak know that the world has left the train behind, that there are better, faster, cheaper ways to travel, but they seem to have collectively decided that they do not care. This is their culture, and they are sticking to their guns.

The train belies the myth of progress that says, "The bigger and faster the better!" It's become the opposite of its original intent: in this racing world, it slows people down. In the observation car, Oren and I pass long stretches of time in amiable silence, with nowhere else to be and no one we'd rather be around. I find myself simultaneously disoriented by the change of pace, so much slower than my life, and longing for it. Flying is disorienting in the opposite way. Landing in a new time zone and climate and culture after only hours airborne, there's a sense of the world folding in on itself, a collapsing of distances. On the train, every mile is on display through the omnipresent windows.

As we near our destination I finally get a chance to write for an Amtrak employee, one of the observation deck stewards, a young black man from New Orleans who is leaving this route to go back to riding the Louisiana-bound train, the Sunset Limited. I ask him the craziest train story he's witnessed, and he tells me about an army veteran who had a nervous breakdown in the mountains, broke a window, and tried to push his wife out.

"The trees want you!" the deranged man shouted.

It took five staff to restrain the guy and lock him in the entryway. The train was four hours away from the nearest station. For whatever reason, bad cell reception or broken Wi-Fi, the attendant who was at the station when the train got in hadn't gotten the message that there was a psychotic man locked in the entryway. He opened the doors on arrival, and the would-be wife-sacrificer burst out. The deranged fellow jumped in the attendant's vehicle and drove off, but then couldn't figure out how to get the golf-cart-size vehicle off the platform and out of the station. He drove in circles for two hours, while the train stalled on the tracks, keeping the passengers locked in until the sheriffs from the next town over could get there to make the platform safe again.

The attendant is excited telling me this story, but doesn't tell it like an exception to the rule of what usually happens on the train, just an extreme instance. Trapped in a sardine tin for days on end, it would be easy to lose touch with the outside reality. I can imagine going crazy in here too.

By day three on board the train, we are all showing signs of physical wear. I break down and try the coffin-size showers downstairs, water hitting me limply as the train lurches from side to side. There's no way the Orens of the world could manage in here, and so as the days go on his forehead plays host to a growing mass of dead skin cells, like the skim on top of milk. It's disgusting, and as I grow to love the old man, the two of us sticking together in this new world, I am more conscious each day that we are all decaying. In these close quarters, it's just harder to hide.

On the train, my back aches and my butt aches from so much sitting. I catch my inner monologue complaining and remind myself that I'm young and healthy. I can't imagine how the older folks' bodies are feeling, especially those not in the sleeper cars who are spending the nights in their chairs. The thing about Amtrak is, it's not significantly cheaper than flying, so most of these people are not here because they lack another financial option. They have chosen cheerful neighbors and a long view of the country over convenience, even over comfort. There's a subtle different sort of valuing going on, on board the train, a prioritization of the human scale. Here, it's impossible to forget that every mile is rich in human stories, the train's windows playing a three-day-long film of abandoned farmhouses and country roads that shows us the human experience all around us, simultaneously hidden and in plain sight. Our train tickets are our badges of a willingness to suffer, a gladness to suffer, a little bit, to exist at this human scale.

The landscape approaching Chicago is one of tractors and abandoned railroad ties, skyscrapers and chemical smokestacks. Utilitarianism is in our blood, it's our watchword. But our land, oh the land, is beautiful. Mile-wide rivers, gorgeous plains.

Dori, the writer from the observation car who offered to write me a poem in return for one of mine, returns to the observation car after lunch with a poem for me and *her* two books. She's from California's Central Valley and is working with some friends on ten acres in Monterey, figuring out how to do sustainable agriculture. Though it seems we're the same age, Dori lives off the social media grid that makes up so much of my life. Her goal is to be the creator, in art as in farming, liberated through a self-sufficiency that my urbanite brain can barely wrap its head around. The idea of writing without gardening is empty to her.

Oren and Dori hit it off right away. "You don't have to make a mark on life to enjoy it," Oren tells her, lost in the memory of his wife. "We had an even life. Uneventful."

"It sounds like you preferred it that way," Dori offers.

"Oh, yes."

Oren finds his poem, which I wrote while he was dozing in the chair opposite me, on the table as I'm writing for someone else. I don't bother reading it to him—even with his hearing aids, there's no way he'd hear it. He and Dori sit across from me and read, in silence, together.

For Oren,

Across the country, again
reliving railroad memories,
same country, fresh faces. We
wound these ways around our fingers
taking home with us, so at the
Grand Canyon, we were home, in
the deserts of New Mexico, home.

Wherever you were was always home.
And now you've gone ahead to get
things ready—you were always so
clever and thoughtful like that—
  and I'll be there, promise
    but for now
I'm riding the rails
    never too old for an adventure
for fresh faces
      and kindness that never
          goes stale.

I watch Oren read with trepidation, afraid of how this veteran
from the Greatest Generation will react to a millennial's unsolicited poem. But when he's done, his eyes tear up.

"Now you've got me crying!" he says, laughing. His eyes meet
mine. "Thank you."

He turns to Dori, proudly, pointing to a line in the first stanza. "See these lines? That's 'cause my wife and I had this RV . . ."

We're near Chicago now, and we return to our rooms to pack. Dori disappears without the possibility of a good-bye, but as we pull into the station, Oren and I leave our rooms across the hall together, for the last time. I help this stranger whom I met three days ago, sitting on my bed, get down the stairs. He refuses to give me his bag until he's halfway down, stubborn and independent till the end.

"The nicest people are those you've just met," Oren tells me. "I'll never forget you." Coming from a ninety-five-year-old man, that means something.

We hug, and I realize it's our first physical contact.

"You go ahead," Oren says, eyeing the long corridor of Chicago's Union Station. "You're faster."

# A Poet at
# the Mall

In March 2017, I responded to a ridiculous post that a friend shared on Facebook: *Apply now! Mall of America seeks Writer-in-Residence to celebrate its 25th Birthday!* Included were a week at the mall, all expenses paid, a public space to write, and a few thousand dollars in cash.

A quick Google search turned up reams of articles skewering the residency as nothing but a shameless publicity stunt, deriding the idea that a writer would come and be inspired by, what, a Nordstrom? And since when, the articles scoffed at the "twenty-fifth birthday" designation, were malls "born"?

"Hey," I thought, "if the Supreme Court says corporations are people, why can't a mall have a birthday? It even has a parent company!" I fired off two paragraphs before bed describing what I did and went to sleep. Like RENT Poet, this seemed like a practical joke. Not something to spend too much time on or take too seriously.

But after a couple weeks I got an email: I was a finalist, one of twenty-five chosen out of 4,300 applicants. I actually had a chance! The email asked for an eight-hundred-word essay detailing what I'd do at the mall, but I wasn't applying to write essays. Instead, I sent in an eight-hundred-word poem as a pdf so I could include unsolicited pictures of the typewriter in action with crowds of adorable children. In corporate America, I understood, even though my product was called poetry, literary merit wasn't what I was selling. I was a photo op, an interactive novelty, and a budget therapist, all rolled into one, though corporate clients usually only learned that last one in retrospect.

The poem with which I sold myself to corporate America ended on these lines:

This vision
is about writing as connection—poetry as a service industry.
This is a vision of poetry as it *can* be,
brought down from the ivory tower
and into the mall, out to the public,
bards spinning tales in Viking marketplaces . . .
What is a mall but the repository
of our collective desire?
. . . And what,
                poetry,
                        but the shortest distance
                        between

feeling                                             and
     expression.

Another email came in, opening with the standard rejection letter lines that by now I was all too familiar with: "Thank you for applying, as you know, we had many strong applicants . . ." But then, and not until the second paragraph, the news: I was in! Suddenly the unnamed benefit of working with a multimillion dollar corporation materialized, and this kid who'd set up a typewriter on the street to hustle passersby for money in exchange for poems, essentially an elevated form of begging, started fielding calls with reporters from the *New York Times* and the *Wall Street Journal* who were intrigued by what secret I had that let me, with my utter lack of qualifications, beat out writers years my senior in age and professionalism to become the mall's first writer-in-residence.

"What secrets does he possess that other writers do not?" the *Times* piece asked.

"Disappointingly normal," it concluded, ". . . just another guy trying to string together enough work to make a living . . ."

I forewent the flights the mall offered to pay for and used Amtrak instead, after ensuring the mall would reinvest my travel money in local artists. The train dropped me off at Union Depot in Saint Paul, with its high columns and yellow walls, and I Ubered to the hotel, which sat just off the mall's premises. The Uber wound around the mall's huge, dark hull for many blocks before reaching the small hotel. Grateful and exhausted from travel, I grabbed a late-night snack at the adjoining IHOP and tumbled into bed. What the next day would hold I could not know.

The next morning, I woke up with all of my anxieties bubbling to the surface at once. "You'll find we are *very* hospitable," my contact at the mall had told me, over and over again on the phone until it sounded like a threat. What, I wondered, would it look like to screw up a writer's residency at a mall?

I got lost exiting my hotel in the maze of corridors. Frantic Muzak accompanied me down hallways that all looked the same, my footsteps echoed by deranged violin music. The hotel, the mall, even the adjoining IHOP, all seemed to have broken free of time and place to exist as a universal constant, almost a platonic ideal. This same Carlton hotel, this same IHOP, are everywhere and nowhere at once, a parade of different faces sliding across identical designs. These places are secure in the promise of sameness, a known quantity providing comfort in this vast and terrifying world.

Opening the door to the outside, a wave of midwestern humidity hit me, a baptism by sweat. It drenched the burgundy dress shirt and jeans I'd agonized over wearing this morning, wanting to seem sensible and relatable but also professional and just a little bit flashy, the way you want an artist to be. In the interminable parking lot, I passed the smallest child, walking backward behind his father. He was being dragged by his tiny hand toward IHOP. I felt a lot like him, in that moment.

A highway wrapped around the mall on all sides like the moat of a fortress island. There was a skyway to get over it, but the glass tunnel was built for snow and had no air-conditioning for the midwestern summer. I walked above the cars like crossing a river, wading through a current of unbearable heat. I half expected a ferryman to appear, demanding two coins for the passage between worlds.

The Mall of America is several city blocks of shopping, four stories high in a long rectangle wrapped around a central hub. As I walked through the bleached white corridors of the outer circle, I caught a glimpse, between stores, of another world inside—a Jurassic Park of fake trees and mountains, giant cartoon heads and roller coasters rising up from the retail at the mall's core. Children screamed like crazy on whirring carnival rides in front of me, all steel blades and flashing green lights. The floor itself changed as I walked, reflective tile giving way to pathways through hills of color between the ferns, speckled with benches and statues. Compared to the sterile shopping space, the theme park interior was a jungle.

Back before the mall was built, twenty-five years ago, this wild interior was the Minnesota Twins' baseball field, and as I walked, nods to that history peeked through like half-buried archaeological relics. A lone red chair survived, high up on the wall. A baseball diamond had been sunk into a walkway where players used to slide into home plate to the cheers of adoring fans.

When I meet the Mall of America team, a few minutes later, I ask them if any of the original architecture from the baseball field was repurposed for the mall. I imagine a skeletal baseball stadium behind the shops and roller coasters, carrying on the building's legacy as an all-American shrine for family and communion.

"No," Dan, the head of PR, tells me, "it was all torn down to the ground."

Dan is older, with gray hair and a calm disposition that hints at quiet power. Two other team members are with him, Chris and Sarah, who turn out to be a married couple who met and fell in love on the job here. Chris does experience design and Sarah is Dan's number two in PR. Chris is a big guy in his midthirties with a toothy grin, the kind of guy who doesn't surprise me in the slightest when he tells me he lived in LA for ten years working on horror movies. Sarah is the kind of woman who walks the corporate tightrope in meticulous makeup, simultaneously soft and commanding, and above all Minnesotan to the core. She introduces me to the phrase "Minnesota nice" to describe her extreme politeness and hospitality.

But the first thing the mall team tells me when I meet them is, "You have to take a picture on the slime chair!"

I grin and nod like this is a normal thing for someone to say, and try to shut off the little voice in my brain that keeps asking, dubiously, *Slime?*

It's midday by now, and the light spilling through the mall's skylighted ceiling reflects blindingly off the walls and polished floors. We head into the maelstrom of screeching children at the amusement park heart of the mall. The slime chair turns out to be a bulbous green plastic bench, built to look like Nickelodeon slime frozen mid-splat. I can almost see the grease of a thousand children who've sat on it, locked in a daily struggle with the mall's team of North African cleaners in their hijabs.

The mall PR team ceremoniously pull out their cameras and instruct me to sit, making me the focal point of this bizarre welcome ritual. I've only perched on the slime chair for a moment when—it talks!

I jump a foot in the air. Recovering, I look up at Chris and Dan and Sarah, who are laughing and congratulating each other.

Now I understand firsthand what an experience designer does, Chris comes over and helps me up with a big smile. Here, he explains, is his pride and joy. The voice that surprised me was one of thirty sound effects he'd programmed, emanating from deep within the plastic hulk. What I'd heard was a rumbling, nonsense garble that was gone as abruptly as it had begun, but he'd also randomized vibrations and gusts of wind, triggered by anyone sitting on the seat, to surprise unwary picture-takers into genuine reactions.

"Five of the effects are fart noises." Chris giggles, like he's gotten away with something. He gleefully recalls watching a kid sit, to the sound of a huge one letting it rip, prompting him to jump and his mom to go off on him. "I didn't do it," the little boy insisted to his scolding mother, "it was the chair!"

"That went over about as well as you'd expect," Chris says, chuckling.

It turns out that this hunk of plastic is more than a farting chair, it's a centerpiece in the vision this group has for the mall. Over lunch, Chris tells me his desire to rebrand the Mall of

America from a "mall" to a "themed entertainment destination." The phrase physically hurts me, but I understand what he means. In 2017, you don't *need* to go anywhere to get *stuff*. "The great challenge of retail spaces now," Chris tells me, "is to create experiences you want to have with other people."

We talk about how space itself can perform and can get people to perform in different ways. In contrast to the placelessness of the hotel and IHOP, the Mall of America is bucking the trend of malls closing by investing in giving people unique experiences that fill in the spaces between identical franchise shops. The slime chair photo op is something Chris fought hard for and is able to hold up as a mark of success for his new model. It's not a ride, it's not generating revenue, but it makes a day at the mall into more of a story. How do you put a number value on that? Chris's job is to remind the higher-ups that every visitor needs to come away with the story of a flesh-and-blood experience, if the Mall of America wants to remain relevant in this instant-gratification, online world. He says he's constantly fighting to carry over these types of experience elements from the amusement park into the rest of the bleached-white retail space of the mall, but it's a frustrating process to get there.

I had wondered why I was here, but now I knew. My role for the next five days was to be the latest chess piece in this battle for the driving vision of the Mall of America. I would be the Farting Chair, Phase 2.

For five days, this was my setup: each day, for four hours, I'd be stationed at a different place in the mall. I'd arrive at the standard-issue mall-white table and chairs and set up my typewriters—a teal Olivetti for myself, and a Smith Corona I'd painted orange-yellow and decorated with roses, which I kept facing outward as an invitation for kids to try a typewriter for the first time. I would write poems for a hundred people who came up to me and answered the question, *What do you need a poem about?*

Every time I write for strangers in public, I'm nervous. I always wonder: Will this be the time, the place, where no one wants a poem? But even at the mall, when we set up to take photos, people stopped, and I breathed a sigh of relief. Poetry *would* work, here, next to Wetzel's Pretzels. When a middle-aged woman just passing by learned that I was writing poems based on any topic people gave me, she barked, "My word is Disney!" so quickly and aggressively that I jumped. We were just doing photos, I hastily explained, I wasn't writing yet.

The first person I wrote for was Dan, the head of PR and my de facto boss during my time at the mall. He was the one, I found out, who'd read each of the 4,300 applications for the writer-in-residence competition, though the employee who had the idea in the first place had somewhat ominously been sacked for being "a bad fit." While I couldn't escape the knowledge that Dan was feeling me out as I wrote for him, judging if he'd made a good gamble on me as the spiritual successor to the farting chair, he started things off with a surprising burst of vulnerability.

Dan wanted a poem about his son, Bryce. Bryce was a father himself now, to a little boy named Franklin, and this poem would be part of Dan's gift to Bryce for Father's Day that Sunday. Dan told me about a trip to Disney World for his fiftieth birthday that his son had surprised him with, about raising a kid as a single dad and his hopes that the next generation would do better than he could. He and his son share a love for Disney, he told me, those Florida vacations a point of easy intimacy in a world where grown men are rarely allowed to show their feelings to one another. When I asked their favorite Disney story, Dan said, "Peter Pan."

The boy who never grows up.

I'd never been a Disney kid. Though I grew up just an hour from Disneyland in California, my one trip there as a kid with my mom was a disastrous slog through heat and endless lines, ending with us getting stuck on the It's a Small World ride for forty-five minutes in the aftermath of the 1994 Northridge earthquake. We'd never gone again. Because my hippy parents refused to allow a TV set into our house, I even missed out on the perpetual loop of Disney classics on VHS that acted as surrogate parents to raise so many of my generation of peers. Suffice it to say, I did not understand Disney.

But I at least knew the story of Peter Pan, and I had some ideas about dads. My own parents stayed together as all of my friends' parents got divorced late in elementary school, and my favorite memories of my dad are of him walking me to school and answering my rapid-fire questions with an academic's patience and deep knowledge until, teenaged and disgruntled, I made him stop. My relationship with my parents had frayed in college, and a big part of what I'd been doing in the past few years was reconnecting with them through small gestures, little allowances that I could still be the kid I'd been to them, even all grown up.

I digested everything Dan told me, through the typewriter, while he watched, into this poem:

For Bryce,

Who never stopped believing in
            faeries, even when all the evidence
                        pointed in the opposite direction—
we were lost boys, both of us, growing
up together (despite our best
intentions). Nothing gives me more
pride than seeing you with
Franklin, taking the time
            to teach him to fly.

Every parent's wish
is for their kid to
grow up to be better
than they were. As
you begin your journey
into fatherhood,
            I am beaming.

We have faced our crocodiles—
            they will not stop us
            from coming back for more.

There is no one
I would rather
not grow up with
    than you.

I was about halfway through reading the poem out loud when Dan started to tear up. All of his staff was gathered around, with a camera crew from the local news station to boot, and this silver-haired man, who was the reason I was here in the first place, just bawled and hugged me and disappeared.

Day one, I'd made my boss cry, and he liked it.

But Dan wasn't the last person to cry in front of me outside of Nordstrom. The mall team was keen that I track certain metrics so that they had fun facts to share on social media: number of poems written, number of steps walked around the building's cavernous interior. After my first day writing, I started keeping another tally—the number of people who cried. It happened every day, like clockwork: four or five people would come away from our interaction with water streaming down their faces, weeping openly in front of the Lego store.

In the end, 20 percent of all the people I wrote for in the mall wound up in tears.

When people come to a mall, especially this mall, they come to scratch an itch. People come to the Mall of America with intention. They are looking for something. Sometimes it's ice cream, sometimes clothing, and sometimes it's just reconnecting with family. Old folks who come for exercise in the morning give way to afternoon shoppers and diverse families in the evening, tourists and immigrants alike indoctrinating their kids in Americana. Everyone's in a special state, somewhere between empty and full, invisible and seen. The mall boasts that it's the number one tourist destination in the Midwest, with forty million annual visitors. It might not be "The Happiest Place on Earth," but it's big enough to be "of America."

I got to know the rhythm of the mall, the midday heat and warmth of skylights, the late-night buzz around closing time as the energy shifted and the teenagers came out. I explored every floor, peeking around "Under development! Sorry for the inconvenience" signs and looking through opaque windows in out-of-the-way corners to see kids smashing into one another on bumper cars. But mostly it was families, tourists and locals alike, shopping and eating and shouting for each other across the mall's vast expanse.

When I stalked the corridors with just my notebook, scribbling observations, it earned me no end of skeptical glances from families and shoppers—What could this dude be writing about? Us? This was a place for experience unshaded by critical reflection. I was a poor spy, and Middle America shrank away from me and my notebook.

But behind the typewriter, when people knew for certain that I was writing about them, I transformed from spy to priest. I wrote a poem for a mother with a stroller who told me that the only way to get her baby to stop crying, when he was a newborn, was to come to the mall. She'd come with her mom, or with her friends, and they'd walk the gleaming halls with the stroller. The constant hum of people and Muzak somehow soothed the baby.

As the temporary darling of the mall's publicity machine, pilgrims began to search me out. If the farting chair gave people genuine surprise and laughter, I acted as a pressure valve, providing emotional release for five minutes at a time. Some people came back day after day.

There was a high to writing in the mall, the complete saturation with humanity, the laser focus on one person after another. Empathy became addictive, beautiful moments stacking up, gift giving and gratitude and people crying. People started bringing gifts themselves, making offerings, and gaining absolution: "I read about you in the *Star Tribune*," or "I saw you on the TV." They brought me their own poems, their photographs, newspaper articles they'd clipped out which they thought might interest me, handwritten lists of places I should go to write, birthday cards because they'd heard it was my birthday. Sometimes, the patrons didn't cry, just me. There was something evangelical about it, my big tent revival.

Some of the people tell me about other pilgrimages they've made, Tibetan meditation retreats to concerts in other countries. A young Korean American woman asked for a poem about her favorite Korean pop star. "My sister and I have been in this fandom for ten years," she tells me. "As a poor college student, I spent all my money to get to Hong Kong and Hawaii for concerts." There's a comfort, she says, in admiring someone so much that you'd literally cross oceans to see them for two hours. Another woman stopped by a few days later with a story about a solo three-day trip to California to see her K-pop crush, where she'd spent thirteen hours in the sun arguing with security, finally breaking down in tears mid-concert at how simultaneously worth it and not worth it the whole experience had been.

"I just finished a weeklong silent Buddhist Tibetan meditation retreat," a young elfin woman tells me. She's waited for thirty minutes to get to me in the bleached interior of the mall. "You learn a lot about yourself, not talking. It's surprisingly full of ups and downs, chaos and nothing. I think I'm in the habit of being rigid. I need to lighten up, to know there will be space and time. It finished at noon today . . ." She trails off. Then: "This is the most talking I've done in a week."

"May I ask, what brings you to the mall?"

She laughed.

"I came to get ice cream at Dippin' Dots to celebrate!"

*We are all this messy contradiction*, I wrote for her, on my clacking Olivetti Lettera 32. Another woman brought in photo after photo of her son and cried just looking at them with me. My role, I quickly realized, was just to grant people permission to express the emotions they kept under wraps in order to get along in public space. The people who come to the mall seem to have this terrible longing to speak and be listened to, to be witnessed. A base, human need to break from the constant impersonal bombardment of consumer culture that lives in that space and to sit, in silence, with a stranger who was there explicitly to care about their stories.

From my perch at the typewriter, I gathered intel on the human condition from the belly of the beast, and the heart of American consumerism turned into a confessional. Lots of people would ask how much my poems cost—in a citadel of commerce, unless the free thing is a sample to lure us into buying, nothing is free. But I wasn't selling a product, I was selling the humanity of the mall itself.

The mall was an unlikely site for love, but slime chair mastermind Chris and his wife, Sarah, Dan's number two in PR, met here. This was where their relationship started, a romance that blossomed through a shared love not of shoes but of stories.

"What connects everyone who works here is passion," Sarah told me, and "all the staff are family." Her words seemed like a corporate mantra, if there ever was one. But only at first. At dinner, Dan shared his story about hiring her, about how she'd worked all over the park in minimum wage positions, temping on this project and interning there, persisting. In this millennial world, to work somewhere, the key I'd found was not to have the best credentials, but to cling to the targeted employer and refuse to let go. The word *passion* scared me for what it revealed about the deeply held convictions corporate employees are required to hold.

Especially in white-collar jobs, it seemed it no longer was enough to simply do a job, people were required to *love* their jobs. When I worked in the nonprofit world, I remember giving my organization's elevator pitch like I was talking about myself at mixers and galas and even just to friends. Maybe there's something millennial about feeling the need for a job to be not just a job, but an identity. As a poet I was an independent service provider, separate from the corporate world that paid many of my bills. I didn't have to love any of my clients, but I was doing the same thing, not with a company but with an art form. I couldn't just write poetry, I had to *be* poetry.

For poetry to fulfill this identity niche didn't seem so strange. If I invested all of my identity in poetry, it was because nothing felt better, more cathartic, more necessary in my life. Surely a mall couldn't provide that—could it? I wondered if my love for poetry couldn't be the same feeling of necessity that Sarah clearly felt for her workplace, what made her decide to fight her way up from entry-level employee to the face of the megacorporation.

There was a homemade quality to the Mall of America, from the giant Paul Bunyan log ride to the slime chair. I'd been afraid that the team would be corporate drones, but they were star-crossed lovers and single dads, and they loved kids and roller coasters because they were kids themselves. In a world that's spinning too fast, sometimes you need a thousand pounds of high velocity metal to slow a family down enough to appreciate it.

"Here in Minnesota," Sarah told me, "it's common for couples to have a cabin on a lake that they go to."

"Disney is *our* cabin," Chris rejoined, in the way couples have of finishing each other's sentences, and told me about all the trips they'd made to the mother of all amusement parks, pilgrimages for every life milestone. "We have a ritual," Chris said, "every time we leave Disney, of taking a picture waving good-bye to the castle together."

Chris's desk was crowded with action figures. Sarah invited me, off-work hours, to a barbecue they were hosting, but it ended up overlapping with my other duties. As I neared the end of my time in the mall, they came to me over and over again for poems— for their fathers, for each other, for themselves.

Chris had fatherhood on the brain with Father's Day coming up. He told me about choosing to spend quality time with his son riding roller coasters at the mall. The first time he'd taken the boy on the Paul Bunyan ride (a very wet canoe experience complete with a giant, ax-wielding statue, as I learned firsthand), the kid had been terrified. "Why is he so angry?" he kept asking. Chris and his son were alone for a long time before Sarah was in their lives, and Chris still worries about raising a son to be both strong and tender, to have an open heart without being afraid. He told me about the awesome responsibility of having a child, of hearing his own words come out of his growing son's mouth.

For Chris,

Fathers on roller coasters learn to be gentle,
defenders against Paul Bunyan
trying to answer, "why is he so angry?"

Because life is hard?

But we learn compassion
tasting our own words
from our children's mouths,
realizing our importance
    if only because we are always building
        the worlds we want to see and those
    we don't, with our own words,
repeated ver batim
an octave up.

Our own words
are no longer our own.
The lessons we try to impart
    about sharing, about being kind.
We are learning  as much as teaching
        with every passing day,
breaking the barriers of manhood
    that have been calcified between us and love.

We face the giant for all of us
and we do not tremble.

    Sarah and Chris talked about finding each other, at last, after tough times, a relationship that blossomed despite painful reminders of the past. "Battle scars mean you've survived," Chris said. He was a single dad raising his son, now a green-haired ten-year-old from a previous relationship, until he met Sarah. Sarah's relationship with her own father was strained. Sarah and Chris had lifted each other up from low points in their lives.

Chris told me that they are their own worst enemies, struggling against the self-doubt they carry. They had a pressed earnestness when they invited me to their family barbecue. What emerged was a realness constructed through fandom, not as a distraction, but a weapon and a shield against the painful vicissitudes of family drama and divorce and the loneliness of drowning in a grown-up world.

The goal of the mall wasn't just entertainment, what Sarah and Dan and Chris and the whole crew were trying to create, by making each mall experience a story, was *feeling*.

As the mall reached the end of its day, I made my way to Nickelodeon Universe to catch the end-of-day light show, designed to make getting through a day at the mall feel like a celebration. Chris talked about the challenge of programming a light show with a glass ceiling under an airplane flyway, trying not to blind pilots.

Under the dancing lights, elementary age kids with faces painted like skulls jerked and cavorted while smoke rose from the ticket booth. A woman's voice that sounded like it was ripped straight out of an animated kids' movie crooned a pop song: "We're always here—always *heeeeeere* for you!"

At the end of every day, the mall closed with this light show and song. "We're always *heeeeere* for you."

When the Mall of America was being built (or born, depending on who you ask), a woman named Sarah Donovan made arrangements to have little chip readers placed at the northern entrance. At the time, this was an impressive feat of technology. Donovan was a healthy-living advocate, and the chip readers let people who wanted to come walk in the mall log the amount of time they walked by swiping their pass when they entered and left the building. Every so many hours of walking, the computer system would award them with a star, releasing a little shot of dopamine in their brains. It made coming to the mall a game that incentivized people to exercise more, the way you might give a mouse a pellet for finding the right path through a maze. The card was called the Mall Stars Walking Pass, and thus the Mall Walkers were born.

Mall of America was one of sixty malls that participated in this initiative, twenty-five years ago. The program had faded and died in every other mall, a holdover from both the Time Before Fitbits and Back When Malls Were Relevant. But the Mall Walkers of Mall of America are still going strong, a geriatric army of over one thousand people a month. They come to pace the fluorescent corridors in the mornings, before the shopping crowd arrives. Usually, they buy no more than a cup of coffee.

I get up early on my second day at the mall to meet the Walkers.

Like everyone telling a fitness story, they are full of testimonials. Mike tells me proudly that he came in at 244 pounds and is now down to 185, while one of the guys from his veterans' group (that meets at McDonald's) was able to get off his heart medication and diabetes pills, thanks to the walking. The Walkers have become a self-contained community, with monthly breakfast meetings featuring a speaker who either talks about health or what's going on at the mall. These things are one and the same for the Mall Walkers. They come every day, rain or shine, and the average age in the group is seventy-five years old.

Judy tells me that she and her husband are moving from a house to a condo, "after twenty-nine years there, we're moving to Applewood to be close to the mall."

"We should catch a ride on that Segway," I overhear one Walker say.

"Would my Fitbit register if I did that?" her friend replies. It's all about the points.

The Walkers I talk to brag that some of their number sport oxygen tanks, while others have dementia, but whatever their ailments, only death stops these troupers from circling the linoleum halls at their own pace. In the Christmas season, the mall even hires the Walkers to act as greeters, taking people to stores they can't find. Much of the conversation, looping around the mile-long track of shopping, is about how the stores have changed over the years, one chain replacing another to alter the landscape.

Deanna has been a Walker since the beginning, twenty-five years ago. Burger King used to open early for the Walkers to get coffee, but not anymore. Nordstrom also used to host the Walkers, she tells me, but since a change in management they've been displaced again. "It was a beautiful spot," she remembers wistfully, "because you look out over Ikea! It's almost outside." Deanna runs a children's music school in town; she is educated and passionate, and talks about getting a hug from Yo-Yo Ma, years ago. We're taking a break from walking to get coffee, which stretches imperceptibly and luxuriously to over an hour.

In the winter, with Minnesota snows, it would be impossible for the Walkers to exercise outdoors. But even in the spring and summer, when the "Land of Ten Thousand Lakes" is singing with greenery, many prefer the even terrain and feeling of safety they get at the mall. They have become an essential part of this place, the eyes and ears of the mall in the morning. Whenever anything is out of order, management hears about it from the Mall Walkers first.

While the Walkers are always noticing their numbers thinning, members disappearing into old age, they notice it casually. So-and-so hasn't been in weeks, or that couple stopped coming a year ago. They comment on these disappearances with something beyond the natural ease old people have talking about death, being surrounded by it, and it isn't accompanied by specifics or grief. It isn't until much later that I think maybe the casualness has its roots in anonymity. Most of these Walkers don't know each other very well, just by sight, by *hello*s as they loop around the infinite track of the mall.

On the third meeting of every month, the Walkers celebrate

that month's birthdays, and there was one woman everyone knew. Winnie Strobles was the resident birthday card writer, and she was at every meeting. She died in 2016 at ninety-seven or ninety-eight. The position of card writer was important and impossible to replace, though they did their best without Winnie. She was the one who knew everyone's birthdays and cared enough to do something about it. The one who'd know when someone was gone.

Jill, the gardener who's taken care of all the mall's plants for the past seventeen years, told me she'd sought Winnie out to copy out, by hand, a poem a man had once written for Jill—Winnie's calligraphy was that good. Days later, Jill would find the table where I'm writing to show me the framed poem, in its neat, Gothic letters, which she'd brought from home. Mall Walker Dan and his wife made a special trip to the mall to find my writing table and to get a poem for Winnie's daughter, Wendy. Even though Wendy lived far away, they said, she'd always come to the mall to help her mother walk.

By the time she died, Winnie had logged nine thousand miles.

For Wendy,

We walkers trace out
history in its rotation,
the end and the beginning
meeting in our steps.

Each footfall is a memory
of Winnie, and so she
echos through the mall
every morning,
every birthday, cards flock
to join her handwritten
notes, new companions
for a woman who could
never have too many friends,
the matron of her tribe—

We walkers
knew your mother
in her final years as our
dear friend, and while she
called you Popcorn for how
you bounced, she had
a spring in her step
through her final days, and
here we are, just trying
to keep up—walkers

circling in her memory.

Even as I transform a different corner of the mall each day
with my presence, it transforms me. My skin, which I'd foolishly

neglected to sunscreen up the week before my residency, starts to peel while I write in front of the Lego store. I molt and grow a new skin, there under the fluorescent lights. Ironically, in doing what it does best—market and sell things—the mall launches my artistic career to a new level. I leave with more publicity than I ever had before, but I'm only there for a week, and when I leave, the mall continues, poetry or not. The experience may be intimate for each person, but the institution remains impassive. A "repository of our collective desire," I called it in my application—all things for all people.

At my typewriter at the end of a day's writing, I meet two young native people from different indigenous tribes, Missy and Josh. Missy is a filmmaker in Minneapolis, while Josh lives on a reservation and works in a public health nonprofit. They've just come from a retreat, which is why Josh is in town, part of a spiritual movement for native people to connect with plant medicine and sacred uses of tobacco. "It's about finding out where we became cracked and teaching us to be generous," Missy tells me.

"I feel beat down in a good way," Josh says. "You know you did the good work if you're totally exhausted—the work that's transformative. The work that's taking care of each other, of my ancestors, my people, my future generations.

"But it's hard to remember how to take a breath for ourselves," he says.

Across the river from Mall of America in Saint Paul, earlier that same day, Philando Castile's murderer was acquitted, and still, black lives did not matter in America. A lot of Missy and Josh's friends are at the protests this evening, but, exhausted from a week of activist work, these two are taking a break at the mall.

They came because Missy saw a cute top at Zara that she wants, and then they're going to get food. As a retreat from collective struggle and harsh reality, the mall becomes a place to treat yourself. You can leave your hardships at the door. It's a celebration where the individual becomes the consumer, with the god-like power to fulfill any need by buying. Here at the mall, people reclaim power and agency over their lives and emotions. Hungry? Get chocolate. Sad? Get wine. Bored? Ride a roller coaster!

Exhausted from a week of deep spiritual meditation? Come to the mall, I guess.

The average amount spent per visit is $163, according to the mall website. The cycle of fulfillment and emptiness which this kind of consumption provides has been so thoroughly explored that it's become a cliché.

But beyond being a place to buy, the mall gets people out of the house and changes their mind frame. People come to the mall to share space with other people, friends and family rubbing elbows with complete strangers and finding common cause in public, in a world that's increasingly privatized. The mall is surprisingly packed with Muslim women in hijabs and Indian families in saris and bindis, all chatting gaily in English. The sharp divisions of race in America don't disappear, but individuals gain a level of anonymity in plain sight here, watching humanity go by. There's a comfort in this anonymous sharing of the mall, a sense that everyone there is part of something bigger, some grand American ideal that may or may not even exist anymore. Even Missy and Josh, demanding fair treatment and tribal autonomy in this America, blend in to become a seamless part of it here.

Surrounded by shop windows screaming to buy products and ride queues screaming to buy experience, people, untamable as always, build their lives.

For Missy and Josh,

Beat down in a good way
carrying the weight of
myself, my ancestors, my
future generations, how
do we remember to take
     breath?


    To be there for the past
brave in the face of trauma
resilient in adversity
and this too is an ancestral
weight. You know
you did the good work if
you're totally exhausted,
    because sometimes it's only
    at the end of the line that
    we can start writing

new beginnings, tobacco
and ink as healing tools
as calls or conduits
to myself, to be with
myself, with all of me, to
     find the space and time in
this bleached world for
a breath for myself.

Missy and Josh had come to the mall to disappear, to be mall people for a moment. It's the end of my writing day, and I talk with them for a long time before I start hammering ink into paper. Mostly, in the poem, I just repeat what they tell me, finding the poem, word-for-word, from our conversation, setting what they've said to a rhythm.

They hold each other and cry for a long time. The tears approached with the inevitability of a tidal wave, at the typewriter, like permission to take that breath for themselves.

I tell Missy and Josh that, apart from a Wetzel's Pretzel, I haven't eaten all day.

"Good, you've been fasting," Missy tells me. I guess it's all a matter of perspective—one man's hunger is another's spiritual enlightenment.

They take me out for dinner and won't let me pay because it's my birthday the next day. I didn't set out to spend my birthday at the mall, it just ended up being the best week to come out and I've never been big on celebrating. Another of Missy and Josh's

friends joins us after dinner, a big quiet guy, who also came to the
city for the retreat. Missy is worried he'll be overwhelmed by all
the people, being from a small reservation.

She suggests we leave the mall to go for a drive. (The next day,
my employers will be horrified that I got into the car with strangers.) It's my first time out of the mall in days, and I understand
acutely why dogs stick their heads out of car windows. I feel like
I've just gotten off a spaceship. The Twin Cities in summertime
are lush, skyscrapers rising off in two directions behind verdant
forests. The sun is setting as we leave the mall, glinting off the
front entrance, and I realize I've never seen the front of the mall
before. It's a collection of giant statues of its own logo and shining
facades of glass, a photo op designed for people arriving at the day
lots by car.

Missy plays tour guide as we drive, and we go down to the
river to see the site where thirty-eight natives were executed at the
gallows on a sacred island. Everything is so green and leafy that
we just catch a glimpse of the old fort, the bend in the river where
the gallows stood, before they pass behind thick trees. The Twin
Cities are full of sacred sites, which become a blur from the car.

Shadows grow long. Night falls.

Missy explains how the Mississippi River reflects the Milky
Way and so becomes a path to the other world.

We stop to get out of the car outside a native housing complex. It's a cookie-cutter apartment building whose identifying
marker is a mural that covers one entire wall with the faces of two
tribes. We talk origins and religion and city living and reservation

living, and they tell me about treaty rights and documentary making and the family nature of small-reservation tribal politics, and I tell them about my experiences living in Scotland and LA, and it feels connected and beautiful. It feels like community.

I arrive back at the hotel built into the mall at midnight, just in time to turn twenty-eight years old. The spell of the mall is broken. It's as if, by going outside, I've penetrated a bubble. The mall no longer seems infinite. The world is larger than this place, even if this place in so many ways is a microcosm of the world. It's a place for broken families to mend, for old folks to remember they are not alone, for everyone who's felt othered or isolated to come be part of the seething consumer mass that is the promise of America. The desire of consumers is increasingly not for *stuff* (they can get that online!), but for a shared experience.

And the mall, that shapeshifter, that house of mirrors, is doing its best to oblige.

# Not In It for
# the Music

Derek was from Seattle and lived in LA, where they'd followed an old girlfriend. They were an aspirational house music DJ and worked during the day as an Uber driver. Derek had been on a college improv team, and every everyday scenario was a scene and a game to them. In 2015, as I nervously gripped the handles of the poetry business I'd inadvertently started, they were my roommate. And my best friend.

Derek loved electronic music and all the culture that came out of it. Their nightly escapades seemed legendary to me, and I got my first look at the electronic music culture on the occasions I got to accompany them to illegal underground clubs that went until six in the morning in sleepy warehouse districts. I felt so cool. Like I was an insider. Like I was getting to experience something only a handful of other people would get to see.

Derek's friends didn't just *go* to music festivals, they went because a certain DJ was playing who I'd never heard of. Some of the friends were the DJs or producers themselves, but others were lawyers, or students, or anything really, the variety was staggering.

I knew them only from house parties, but I also knew they met at full-moon parties in the desert, like some secretive cabal, with their own language and geographies. It seemed like everyone had been to Burning Man, some still went to Burning Man, but everyone lamented how corporate it had gotten. Coachella had gone hardcore capitalist, they reported. The feeling of community was increasingly hard to find. A myriad of other festivals passed like currency between their tongues, each with its own reputations and secrets.

I was drawn to the tight-knit community I found through Derek, people from all sorts of backgrounds drawn together by . . . something. How did these music kids figure out how to have so many friends and seem so dang liberated? Derek moved away to Berlin, where the house music scene is legendary, before I could find out.

I felt like an old curmudgeon in his midtwenties, on the outside looking in at what the kids were doing. So when I got the opportunity after my Mall of America residency to go to the Electric Forest music festival and get paid to do it by reading poetry in a secret backstage area, I leapt at the chance. I wanted a little piece of that cool. But I was also cynical about the growing popularity of electronic music festivals, their spiraling price tags, and the various reports of overdoses and sexual assaults taking place in these spaces. I try to be especially cynical about things I secretly really want to do.

On the Amtrak from the Mall of America to Rothbury, Michigan, where Electric Forest is held, I strike up a conversation with the college student sitting next to me to learn that he's from neighboring Flint. We talk about the poisoned water while the train cuts through a landscape of brick stacks belching smoke, freight cars that rust against an iridescent blue-orange sky. In the brutal industrial landscape, the idea of art—even the idea of a forest—seems completely alien.

This train is called the Wolverine.

But the festival is remote, so from the train I have to get on a bus, where I notice a young woman, maybe nineteen, in a baggy wolf T-shirt with a bedroll on top of her pack. "You headed to Electric Forest?" I ask.

"Yes! You too?"

We sit together and within a few sentences agree to split a seedy motel for the night, not so much because we instantly click and are now best friends for life, but because we're both broke and not great advance planners. My new roommate has taken the bus solo all the way from Texas to come to the festival. All her friends flaked, but she's here, covered in tattoos of flying saucers and Harry Potter symbols to remind her not to lose hope. She has anxiety, she tells me, and comes to festivals to let go.

Rothbury boasts a population of 426 which swells to over forty-five thousand people for two weekends a year. A lit-up sign over the McDonald's as we pull into town reads "Welcome Forest Dwellers!"

That night, my new roommate and I check into a hotel where we'll sleep in parallel cots in a room that stinks of cigarettes. But first, we split cheesy, bacon-y tater tots at Denny's, and she tells me that Electric Forest is a pilgrimage for her every year. She works part-time and does odd jobs to save up for this weekend of rough camping, where radical acceptance is the core ethos. In the outside world, she was an outsider, she says, but in this haven of outsiders it feels like she can finally relax and let her guard down. She tells me she doesn't think she'll even do many drugs, this time around: "I've learned everything I've needed to from them." No, she's here for the community. It's a community that turns no one away, she claims.

The next morning, I've arranged to complete my odyssey into the festival in a rented car with two of my new poetry coworkers, who flew in from New York that morning. As I leave the motel where my new roommate lies, still fast asleep, a shirtless homeless man on the sidewalk calls after me: "Get yourself a Cadillac in the name of *Jesus!*" It's a blazing Michigan summer. Squeezing past mounds of baggage into the backseat of the rental with the other poets, I start to get a headache almost instantly from the EDM blasting through the car stereo. Crap. I forgot I just don't get this music. Community, Brian, think about community!

The poet who's driving has eighties hair, a big New York attitude, and monologues in an incessant hipster whine. The other, from Romania, smokes without speaking in the passenger seat. They're both in their midthirties, I guess. Eighties Hair tells me, "The people we met on the plane, coming here, are like, *camping* people. Weird, right? They laughed when I said I'd never been camping before. I mean, I've been once, but I had, like, people who like carried my stuff and brought me hot water in the morning."

"Where?" I ask.

"Oh, that was like in Peru."

I'd read a hundred think-pieces on entitled hipsters taking over music festivals, and like clockwork, here we were.

The Poetry Brothel, where I work for the next two weeks, is a small backstage area behind one of the festival's four main concert areas, intentionally hidden so that only the adventurous find it. To enter it, you have to pass through a big-top tent filled with nostalgic World War II fighter pilot Americana: a station where women and men crossdressing to look like Rosie the Riveter will "buff" you with car buffers on a massage table, a functional barber shop, a bowling alley and poolhall, a bar, a fake sailor tattoo parlor, and a real pie shop. And, of course, a stage for the main event: the music.

But if you turn left at the stage and pass the women in bright blue wigs who staff the pie shop, you come to a fireplace with a typewriter on a shelf above it. To get into the Poetry Brothel, you have to knock at a secret door behind the fireplace and say the password, which turns out to be *consent*. The gaggle of festival kids sweep you into another world, an intimate boudoir of disco balls and velvet-curtained bedrooms where a masked man greets you with an accordion.

"Hello, darlings and lovelies! Do you know where you are?" he says. Stoned silence and confusion are the correct response. "You've reached the shitty part of Narnia! Mr. Tumnus comes here on weekends when he's drunk . . ." He jokes for a few minutes until you are completely unsure what is going on, then reveals that you have in fact discovered "The Poetry Brothel! Gasp!" Yes, he says "Gasp." The emcee asks if you would like to meet the poetry whores. "And it's okay, they like to be called that!" he assures. Strangers in lingerie or suits or headdresses made of tree bark appear, and lead you, still with no answers but now giggling uncomfortably to the people next to you, into a dimly lit back room with a velvet curtain and a soft bed. The whores fill the luxurious beds with grungy festivalgoers and . . . read them poetry.

Young ravers, high on everything from weed to LSD, line up to say "consent" to an empty fireplace, and watch it swing open. I develop a patter for my bedful of strangers, to go with my character: "Some people say, 'RENT Poet, you could have been anything in the world. You could have been an accountant, or a lawyer, or a business executive. Why did you choose this life? Why did you choose to become . . . a *poetry whore?*'"

Pause for dramatic effect.

"I tell them: Some people have a choice. Some people have a *compulsion.*"

And then I read them this simple poem, written on the street years before at a bike event for someone who was afraid of moving and leaving their friends behind. On the muddy bed of the Brothel, between velvet curtains, it becomes a manifesto, a way of trying to translate to kids on a whole lot of drugs just what I'm trying to do with this whole poetry thing:

## I LOVE YOU LIKE IT'S OKAY TO GIVE MY REAL NAME

Sometimes,
just knowing someone
is a way of taking
a little piece
of your soul out of *you*
to send it rushing
down their roads.

To take them
with you.

My heart is a caravan,
my smile,
a welcome mat.

In this giving,
I am able to lose
myself.

I gain only
all of mankind.

"Maybe people are buying personal epiphany," Velvet Envy,
one of the poetry whores, muses backstage while we are getting

our metaphorical (and, in her case, literal) garters off at the end of a shift. "They're trying to fit embodied, communal knowledge into discrete units for their corporate lives. Of course, here, the people are part of the product—what you're coming to the festival to see is each other."

I confess to Velvet that I don't really *get* music festivals, not yet, and at the end of these somewhat academic musings she asks, "Shall we wander in and do anthropology?"

We emerge from the dark of the Brothel into the trees that give Electric Forest its name. The fragrant pines are planted in razor-straight rows and stripped of branches until about thirty feet up. Little about them reads "natural." They are soldiers in file, all the same height. I think the festival organizers must have stripped the branches to hang lights and prevent festivalgoers from climbing them and falling to their deaths. A sign says "Welcome to Sherwood Forest," but I'm skeptical of the Robin Hood reference for a festival with VIP tickets that cost thousands for a weekend of fantasy.

In the middle of the grounds, not near one of the stages but nestled discretely between the trees, sits an old, beat-up four-wheeler. A memorial plaque next to it says WALLY WOJACK, 1927–2017. We stop to watch rave kids still sweaty from dancing pause to leave kandi (cheap handmade jewelry) like an offering at a shrine. Rusty metal disappears under multicolored beads that say things like "peace" and "booty."

A screen mounted on the back of the four-wheeler plays a looped video, a documentary for YouTube attention spans about the rancher in a cowboy hat who "planted Electric Forest." In 1955, Wally Wojack bought the 2,300-acre ranch, devastated by harvesting, and planted it with thousands of six-inch-tall white pine saplings. Sixty-two years later, the trees are over seventy feet high. The land and the festival that happens on it are his legacy.

Festivalgoers cluster around the four-wheeler's screen to watch the old rancher's memory speak. The video shows him grinning from a couch, World War II regalia and Western horse kitsch behind him. "My wife didn't go for all this friendly stuff," he says, and the video cuts to him, still in his cowboy attire, drinking and dancing with nearly naked college-age kids. "I'd come home and she'd say, 'Grow up, Walter, grow up.'"

He reminisces fondly about competing in an adult baby costume contest.

"These kids act like the kids did in the 1950s," he says. "We dressed funny, we drank a lot of beer, and we had fun."

For Wally, the parties were a way of reclaiming a youth lost to World War II. "I grew up fast," he remembers. Those post-war parties were a sort of rebirth after all the destruction, an F-U to death and a celebration of life in all its raw messiness. The kids at Electric Forest would have been three years old when the Twin Towers fell, five when the US invaded Iraq. Their war has never ended. It is the 24/7 news cycle, recruitment centers in strip malls promising a way to *get out*, pickup trucks with American flags and gun racks preparing to defend against an invisible enemy half a world away.

A pair of young men dressed in full camo at the exit to one of the campsites pretending to be soldiers ask our names as we pass by and radio over to their friends to let them know we are "friendlies." It's a sweet gesture. It makes me a little afraid.

Through the neatly planted and stripped trees, I can hear the throb of deep bass. A young man standing next to me at the memorial to Wally Wojack, wearing wolf ears, says to the girl on his arm, "What a man!" Then, more loudly, he addresses the small crowd standing around the four-wheeler, "WHAT A MAN!"

Another boy, face riddled with acne, nods sagely by way of reply. "They don't make 'em like that anymore," he says.

The trees are interspersed with art installations, and we're not more than five minutes in when a stranger approaches and asks if we'd be part of a wedding. I agree skeptically—a few other groups of performers are already standing around a young woman in bridal attire, and at first I think it's a show. There's actually a fake wedding chapel in the middle of the forest, where an absurd preacher does staged weddings where someone always objects. But this wedding is real.

The couple are young and seem sweet, though as a writer I can't help judging their clunky vows just a little bit. "As the circle of the ring completes itself, you complete me," the groom says, slipping a ring on the bride's finger under a giant hummingbird statue made from branches. They met here last year, I learn.

Aside from the minister and one friend, everyone in the audience is a paid festival performer—mimes create a pathway for the bride while faeries, spray-painted gold, frolic and giggle in front of the couple. The one real friend the couple have here snaps a photo, and I think that this is a level of production value that you'd have to spend thousands of dollars to get for a wedding outside the forest. Even so, I can't help but wonder where these people's friends and family are, these young beautiful people getting married in front of a crowd of strangers whose outward happiness is just part of their job description.

"By the power vested in me by the state of Michigan . . ." the minister begins. I gulp. Up until now, the whole thing could have been a show. But no. This is real life, a real binding of two people, transformation and rebirth from two to one.

Afterward, the minister passes out his business cards: "Have Your Wedding in the Forest."

There are too many bands, too many stages and secret experiences to ever come close to seeing it all. This is the hook—because it's impossible to complete the festival, people have to come back year after year, convinced of the unique sacredness of their experience.

Backstage, I joke that Electric Forest is just an avant-garde writers' retreat. In their off time, the other poets sit with headphones writing raps, or wandering with notebooks, weirdos for whom writing is not a choice but a compulsion, people who have that sort of lens over their world. It's like their vision is out of focus until it's set in ink.

During the day at the Hangar Stage, before the DJs play, a mustachioed emcee invites festivalgoers to display their talents as Hula-Hoopers, jugglers, dancers, anything they might desire. It's

Electric Forest's Got Talent, 2017. "Thanks for showing up to support people just like yourself," the emcee says. The point of the talent show, it seems, is to take ordinary festivalgoers and elevate them, momentarily, to star status—just another form of wish fulfillment the space provides. The festival caters to the desires of the stoners and tweakers and ketamine kids, but it knows that performers are addicts too.

Our drug of choice is attention.

The talent show turns out to be an audition of sorts, as many of the performers working here were invited back after being "discovered" as paying attendees at Forest in years past. One of our poetry whores came to us this way, a Hula-Hoop dancer and diehard festivalgoer who goes by Cherry Popper ("Cherry-Popper99@AOL.com," our emcee roars by way of introduction, to the audience's delight). When she's not at the festival circuit that she's made her second home, Cherry Popper is an attorney in Texas who specializes in criminal law. She's defending a man being wrongfully accused of murder, she tells me, and her freewheeling festival persona falls away to reveal hardened passion as she recounts the injustice of the case backstage during one shift.

The token-low pay for our ecosystem of sideshow acts starts to make sense—these are people who would be here anyway. The festival organizers are just giving us what we want, while gaining an invaluable function: the artists create permission for paying festivalgoers to lose their inhibitions and start to perform, themselves. By trying on personas they wouldn't have the freedom or courage to adopt in real life, the non-performers are rehearsing to become the people they want to be: more generous, more kind, bound by the festival culture values of peace, love, unity, and respect.

At the artists' tents, I meet a huge man clad in lederhosen with a thick German accent, which he suddenly drops after a full hour of conversation. Apparently he was just wandering around the festival last year, pretending to be German, when one of the organizers got wind of what he was doing and asked him to come back this year, expenses paid, in exchange for performing at all times. For him, the festival is a place for what I'd call "performance as research," a space to try on characters and bits to get reactions, adjusting outfits and stories to tweak how people respond without the pressure of having to carry a narrative, and with the added benefit of hard drugs.

"I'm here with my girlfriend," Lederhosen tells me, then slides back into his accent. "Ve're about to dwop some acid before ve get back out zere!"

But the line is thin between freedom and the performance of freedom, and not everyone gets to do what they love. Many of the skimpily clad women dressed as stewardesses and handing out free candy are serious professional dancers and singers, who are eager to show off their talents backstage. But in public, their job, what's earned them their staff wristbands, is their ability to smile behind multicolored wigs, look thin, and get high people to buy things.

The Brothel's magician, whose stage name is "The Magic," wears a suit onstage and a T-shirt off of it. Coming back to the tent one night, he says, "I need to put together an outfit so I can interact with these people!" With the intentional blurring of lines between performer and festivalgoer, a guy in an ordinary T-shirt gets passed up by nearly everyone. He just isn't playing the game right. This is the danger of this place, where people come to peacock and be seen—if you stop performing, you disappear.

The Brothel is perfectly situated as a sideshow, the hokey banter and accordion at the beginning, the little rituals of the whores in their private rooms. I start asking audiences in my bedroom readings if they're okay getting a little more (dramatic pause) *participatory*, before asking each of them for a word and stringing them together in an improvised poem. The words range wildly, even in a single session:

"Consent!"

"Umm . . ." after some prodding, "that's all I got."

"Lugubrious." ("Use it in a sentence! Wow, sad or dismal. We do learning here too!")

"Opulence."

"Infinity."

"Mellifluous."

"Boot." "Stars." "Orgasmic." "Fantabulous." "Sanguine."

I tell the audience on my bed, "This poem has never been heard before and will never be heard again—it exists in this space, in this room, between these people. It will contain each of your words, in reverse order. This one has a little bit of a soundtrack," I always say, shouting over the thumping music. "I know it's tough, but if you can imagine some really heavy bass coming through the walls, that'll make the experience way better. Everyone breathe in . . . out . . . here we go!"

Pulsing, pounding, intimate and *sanguine*
my blood rushes through your veins
I want it back
I wanna feel *fantabulous* in your arms
the *orgasmic* circles of the heavens making me see *stars*
I wanna be on Jupiter, plunging my space *boot*
through that gaseous giant.
Ooh *mellifluous* mellifluous wretch of myself!
I threw out perfection like a used cigarette
dusted my shoulders into *infinity* and crowned my head with
   *opulence*
I was a wreath of the *lugubrious*, king and queen in one—
I made them bow before me and we all cried together, we all wept
   openly, we licked each other's tears and said *"um, that's all I got!"*
We found each other, in our sadness as much as in our happiness,
in our leaving as much as in our coming.
Thank you for coming.
Thank you for your *consent*.

I end every performance with a new improvised poem, reveling in the space to create with people, watching their eyes widen as I hit each word. It's an old classic improv game, but I can feel myself getting better at it as I practice, hour after hour, learning to get out of my own way and let my brain go where it will. There's a total release to freestyling. It's like a trust fall. After I finish the freestyle poem, I wait a beat for people to know it's over and clap. Then I ask, in a whisper, "Are you satisfied?"

As they leave, the audience tips me in cash and hard drugs. I sell more books to teenagers on drugs in rural Michigan than I ever sell at literary events in LA. This is my job for six hours a day, Thursday through Sunday, for two weeks.

There's a performance high to working in the Brothel, the thrill of connecting with people, feeling them wrapped around my finger, or the challenge of an unreceptive audience who are too busy trying to find friends, or tripping way too hard to listen to poetry. And there's the glee of soliciting tips at the end, like gambling with the slot machines of druggy pockets.

While the stages and forest feel wildly expansive and boomingly loud, the Brothel is close and tight. It's a space of relative quiet and comfort and intimacy in the midst of it all, Michigan mud and lightning and omnipresent beats. Passing through the space, it seems like people are digesting their experiences on the outside. I do a poem for a tweaker couple, two rail-thin but gregarious young people with big smiles that reveal teeth wrecked by meth. In the main room, they pipe up to tell our emcee that this weekend is the year anniversary of their wedding. "We got married here at Forest last year!" the young woman crows delightedly.

But once we get into the room, she points to a poem in my book called "For Your Father." "My dad just died," she tells the small group, brave and vulnerable all at once, but with no hint of uncertainty. "Read that one!" As I finish the poem (*their dust / is in my fingernails / their voices / on my tongue*) the young bride buries her face in her husband's shoulder and bawls. He comforts her, his gaunt eyes meeting mine from behind long, stringy hair, as he lists their dead in a low, confiding tone. His wife's father is just the latest to leave them, preceded by the husband's brother and other friends of theirs who took their own lives through accidental overdoses at this very festival in years past. The forest is full of ghosts for them, happy and sad.

And it's not just this couple. Everyone I meet is wearing memories of loss on their sleeve, raw and open, though whether because of the drugs or the intentional community, I can't say. At the end of the first weekend, a young guy laments to me as he clambers onto the sheets about the various times his experience here has flirted with ruin. "My mental health has been an issue," he tells me, unbidden, the moment he meets me. The young man's word for his group's improv poem is "Mom," and I freestyle a moment about diving underwater, feeling held by the water, like a mom's embrace. Afterward, he wants to talk. "She just died," he says. When I finally pull the velvet curtains back and tell my room it's time to go, he pauses to tell me, "Coming here, I know it's all been worth it."

Holy Crow, our palm reader and resident witch from Salem (*that* Salem), talks one-on-one through the night with festival-goers, and when we get off work at 2 A.M., sometimes we trade insights. We are both buzzing with so many people, unable to sleep, sitting together in the big artists' tent. She tells me about a twenty-two-year-old kid whose palm she read, who told her he grew up in a shelter and works in a factory. He came by himself, with his alcoholic mom yelling after him, "I hope you get fired, then you'll learn your lesson!" He took just one day off to be at Forest this weekend, and he can't miss another day at work for the next seven months.

"I'm boring and have nothing to say," the shelter kid told Holy Crow.

Another girl she talked to had deliberately OD'd on coke to try to kill herself. She was just out of rehab and had become a stripper. She told Holy Crow, "I've made it! For the first time in my life, I have a car and money."

"Honestly, she's on a path where she won't make it to thirty-five," Holy Crow tells me, the words gaining gravity, coming from a fortune-teller's mouth. "But I didn't tell her that." The fortune-teller is not surprised that people tell her their life stories but is surprised by the content. "I was expecting a privileged kid playground, and that's not what I got at all," she tells me.

Could it be a rave is just a massive machine to process grief and trauma? In weird ways, these become humanizing forces, explanations of why people are the way they are. Not an apology, just a reason. Maybe the ability to share grief here, without judgment, is what creates connection—"Oh, you're fucked up that way? *Me too.*"

Tallulah Rosa, another poetry whore, who teaches English as second language back in the real world, points out that happy experiences inevitably remind us of our own mortality because we remember people we wish were there with us. Wandering through the forest, I find an area surrounded by lanterns called Reincarnation Village. On the lanterns, festivalgoers have written the names of loved ones. At night, as everyone stumbles back to their tents, the lanterns glow through the trees.

On Sunday, the last day of the festival, before everyone leaves this space to resume their everyday lives, there is a space where hundreds of butterflies are released into the sky.

At the Brothel, our shifts are slow at first. Part of having secret rooms is that no one knows about them. In the downtime we have, various performers collaborate to make a verbal scavenger hunt for clues that people can follow, searching out characters around the forest to eventually gain admittance into the Captain's Lounge, a place even more secret and selective than the Poetry Brothel. I sneak in through the staff entrance, and it turns out to be just another overpriced bar.

But no one knows that before they get there. People go nuts looking for clues, racing between characters and accosting anyone they suspect of being in on the game. Some of the performers who do have clues play along for a few days before being overwhelmed and hiding. They are constantly beset on all sides, interrogated by hundreds of frustrated, even angry people, trying to get access to something. They don't know what that thing is, but it's exclusive, so they want it. It will make them special. It will heal their pain.

A line quickly develops in front of the "secret" entrance to the Poetry Brothel. We have three door people just to hold down the fort, and they are the most beleaguered, constantly in character. Their job is to deny that the entrance exists and keep people from forcing their way through until there is space in the Brothel to fit more. The effect of the door guards is to whip people's acid-trip curiosity into such a frenzy that they start coming around the tent, bypassing security guards and peeking in through the dressing room. They break the hinges on the secret fireplace. They shove against the thin plywood walls that hide the Poetry Brothel from the outside until the walls themselves cave in.

These audiences, so loving with each other, so caring and intimate in the space of the bedrooms where poetry happens, are a ravenous horde when they are on the outside waiting. Every morning, the Brothel needs repairs—we are under constant siege by laypeople so desperate to find something that they will destroy it.

They don't even know that the secret they've been clawing from the walls of this place is just poetry. In my private readings, festivalgoers start listening impatiently, wanting to get on with the poetry, to stamp this experience in their mental festival passports before demanding, "Yeah, but do you know how to get into the *Captain's Lounge*?"

"No," I tell them. "That's something else."

And they're off, screaming futile "CONSENT!" at anything that looks like it might be an opening. I move on to my next group—"Have you ever been poem-ed before? No? *Virgins?* That's okay, we get a lot of first-timers here."

# Drifters:
# Interviews with
# Van Life Poets

Imagine waking up to a different sunrise each morning, over craggy mountaintops or vast expanses of desert. Imagine getting to choose what you did each day. No boss. No work. No schedule. Just the open road. A vast country where you can drive for days on end. Sometimes you'll still wind up in an identical shopping center thousands of miles away, but sometimes you'll float between waterfalls and mountain gorges and the sea. Imagine knowing that you could be anyone you wanted, live a new life in each place. Imagine not being bounded by geography but living everywhere. And sure, maybe it would be lonely sometimes, but surely the trade-off would be worth it. When no one knows your name, you can be anyone, do anything.

The earliest seed of this thought was planted for me in high school, longing to be special in the bleached hallways filled with thousands of jostling children, just doing their time. I was filled with wonder and awe by an upperclassman, eighteen to my fourteen, who had just gotten back from traveling on his own for the first time and seemed so confident and independent to my opening adolescent eyes. "Did you ever give people a fake name or pretend to be someone else?" I asked him.

"No," he told me. "On the road, I felt like I was the most honest I've ever been. There was a feeling of not ever having to worry if people would like you or what you said. You'd be gone the next day, so it didn't matter. At home, I'm performing all the time. Traveling, I didn't have to worry about anyone else. I was just me."

Crisscrossing the country with my typewriter, I started to meet real American nomads, who made me feel like an impostor with my monthly rental to slink home to. At Electric Forest I met Kevin Devany, whose house was a 1994 maroon Dodge Ram van named Martha. The big white clunker opened up into a cozy little kitchen and bedroom for two. Kevin had decked the vehicle out, by hand, with hardwood floors, a sink attached to a water jug with a pump, and a mini-fridge and air conditioner which ran off the solar panels attached to the roof. Kevin was traveling and working with his then-partner, Paeton, and the music festival was just a stop on their never-ending journey. I sat up with them nights as they dreamed about where they'd go next.

Their commitments were few and far between, and other than occasional plane rides home to go visit family they were at complete liberty to spend months in secluded camping spots, emerging every now and then to go busk in town. Kevin wrote poems and Paeton read tarot cards. He was tall and lanky, with a bald head and long pointed beard, always immaculately dressed, while she had wild hair and a nose ring and a cheeky grin. They had friends all over the country, and in some ways van life sounded like a never-ending reunion tour.

"Don't invite us to the party if you don't want to *party*!" was one of their mantras, and their stories of carousing around the nation inevitably ended with them being the last ones at the party, the first to answer adventure's call. With no obligations and no one to answer to but themselves, they lived large and burned madly like Kerouac's fabulous roman candles. I was drawn to them instantly.

"I stumbled on a way to create what and how I wanted to create," Kevin says. "The question of whether it could even be done was a driving factor that made me want to do it." There were practical considerations at play as well. Kevin's life felt like it was falling apart since he had to close his first business, the Art Bar, which was exactly what it sounds like. He wasn't sure what was next, and he was having issues with his landlord, so one day he floated the idea of nomadic van life to Paeton. To his surprise, "she was down."

Kevin had been an avid rock climber and met people through the rock-climbing community who had done van conversions that let them climb for long stretches in the middle of nowhere. "Seeing other people living with that much freedom was attractive," Kevin says, then laughs: "and also a goddamn illusion 'cause it doesn't show the hard parts!"

He says the freedom itself is a challenge. The dark side of self-reliance is that when things go wrong, you have only yourself to blame. "There's no one to tell you where to invest your time, effort, and energy," he says. "Every decision you make is your own fault. There's a huge uncertainty to it. Any time you set up to work in a town there's a chance the cops will just kick you out right away and you'll have to spend hundreds on gas to get to the next city."

In addition to the essentials for living, Martha the van holds a homemade setup: a custom desk with a few drawers and a big umbrella which forms a mobile office space that Kevin wheels out from the van to type. The desk is just the right size for a vintage typewriter, and the sign hanging from a little hook next to it says POEMS.

Kevin tells me, "I like the ambiguity. It means that only the curious come up." This is Kevin's seventh typewriter setup, though he's constantly innovating and improving it. Kevin relies on a mix of government websites and busker community Facebook groups and blogs to try to determine where it is safe for him to set up and work, but laws change frequently and the information is often unavailable or out of date. For Kevin, who both works and lives in public space, just existing there is often a crime.

Kevin has an array of tools he uses to intentionally make himself nonthreatening so the police are less likely to move him along. He is a tall, lanky white man (which itself vests him with privilege) and he dresses this up with a vest, a button-down shirt, a tie, and wingtip shoes. He doesn't list a price anywhere and uses a sliding scale to sell his books and poems. The typewriter itself occupies a weird middle ground, escaping injunctions against musical instruments and sound amplification despite making noise. "The sound holds shared nostalgia for people at an age to be authority figures," he says. The very idea of "poetry" carries with it high-art associations that make people categorize what he does clearly as artistic rather than commercial. When Paeton would read tarot cards across from Kevin while he wrote poetry, she would often be moved along while he was left alone.

"People with strong religious beliefs would think their souls were being threatened by tarot," Kevin says, "but no one feels like poetry is threatening their soul."

"Clearly they haven't read much good poetry," he adds.

"My goal is to re-weird the world," he tells me. Writing poems on the street around the country, the only people he and fellow van life poets have to deal with are those willing to enter an experience that isn't entirely predefined. "We protect ourselves from the unknown out of fear," Kevin tells me.

In a world where online maps tell us the exact amount of time it will take to get somewhere in traffic, and our online libraries of music let us know every song a band will play at a concert, Kevin is trying to open people up to an experience of not knowing that inspires curiosity and compassion rather than fear.

"I meet so many homeless and impoverished people in my work and travels," Kevin says. "It's part of a larger issue—what it means to be in public, and especially to be poor in public, in America." The US Department of Housing and Urban Development doesn't collect data directly on people living in vehicles, but city counts show skyrocketing numbers, particularly on the West Coast. Residents are pushed into their cars due to rising costs of housing in cities from LA (the homelessness capital of the nation) to San Francisco to Seattle, where a 2018 count showed a 46 percent increase in people living in their vehicles from the year before.

There are numerous reasons people live in their vehicles, from chronic homelessness to people deciding to live off the grid to retirement-age folks who trade homes for RVs to explore the country. There's also a diversity of timelines people spend in their cars, with many unreported instances lasting just a few weeks or months as people fall back on living in their cars during times of change and upheaval: after being kicked out of their homes, in the wake of natural disasters, or upon first arriving in a new city.

As cities combat homelessness at the behest of neighborhood associations and business councils, they tighten street regulations and clamp down on self-expression of all kinds on the streets, including the art and street performance that some vehicle-dwellers use to make their living. The National Law Center on Homelessness and Poverty, which tracks laws in 187 cities, reports that the number of prohibitions against vehicle residency nationwide more than doubled between 2006 and 2016. In cities across California and Washington, "safe parking" programs designating specific lots with some amenities for urban car camping are being piloted, with mixed success, trying to corral people into car ghettos whose homes allow them to live literally anywhere.

Kevin weaves his way through my story over the years, and Martha pops up in LA from time to time. She rattles and clanks, struggling to rev up to the speed of traffic on the 101 freeway in LA, at last coming to rest in front of my house on a palm tree— lined street of rundown craftsman homes and student housing for the nearby university. I've told Kevin he's welcome to park in front of mine and make use of my shower while he's here. "Knowing where you're going to use the bathroom in the morning is a rare blessing in van life," Kevin tells me by way of thanks.

Kevin's been on the road for two and a half years at this point. He and Paeton have split up, and he's still reconciling what it means to pursue this life on his own. In conversations over the years after we first met, I gradually learn the less glamorous parts of van life, instance after instance of cops knocking on the door in the middle of the night to move Kevin along. Kevin tells me his biggest enemy is his own biology, which sometimes wakes him up in the middle of the night in a rural area and demands to use the bathroom, even if that means uprooting to drive twenty miles to get to a Denny's and spending precious cash Kevin doesn't really have to get in.

Breakdowns are less common, and Kevin takes pride in doing as much of his repair work as he can himself. He has the two-thousand-page vehicle repair manual ("not the one that comes with the car!" he boasts) that details all of the wiring, every nut and bolt, and proudly shows off the power tools in one of the storage units at the bottom of the van. I ask Kevin if he had any electrical or construction experience before and he tells me no, he's been learning it all as he goes.

He tells me that before he was forced by electrical issues beyond his skill to take the van in for yet another set of costly repairs, he finally called his family to ask for money. "I was able to make that ask," he says, citing his middle-class background. Kevin has both undergraduate and master's degrees in poetry, the student loans from which equal the cost of a house. He cites the impossibility of ever getting out from under his debt as a big reason settling down feels hopeless. "I rarely look as poor as I am," Kevin says. He notes the cruel irony of his poverty—because he is articulate and presents himself as having money, people will stop and give him money for his poems. It's as if he's figured out vagabonding and become its prince.

"My brother just got a job at a first-class investment firm," Kevin says. "Meanwhile, I'm just trying to trade street cred for a house." I'm surprised for a moment. Kevin daydreams about getting a patch of land and building a house with his own hands. "I think I could learn to do that, and I want to," he tells me. Like living in the van, there's a "because it was there" mentality. Kevin says he never plans to have kids (again a quick reference to student debt), so building a physical structure that lasts would be a legacy of sorts.

Plus, Kevin says, "I'm ready for a dwelling I can stand up in." An imposing six foot two or three, he tells me that of all the hardships of van life, the one that gets to him the most is existing in a perpetual state of being hunched over, unable to stand straight.

Like me, many people who take to the road have an end date and never abandon their homes but treat the transitional space of travel itself as a second home. Aryeh-Or Katz took a ninety-day road trip in 2015 after a big breakup, sleeping in his car and writing poetry on a typewriter to get food and gas money. He's a half-black half-Jewish LA native with the classic multi-hyphenate actor/writer/musician/model career, with boom and bust periods of work that make this sort of soul-searching travel possible.

I was there when Aryeh-Or wrote his first poem for a stranger on a typewriter. My group, Melrose Poetry Bureau, was writing out back of a bar and performance venue when Aryeh-Or happened upon us and jumped at the opportunity to use one of the spare typewriters. The next week, he hit the road.

Aryeh-Or is as tall and fashion-forward as Kevin, with an easy air and charm to spare. I ask about travel as a black man in America and he gets serious, telling me he found himself in Cleveland during protests for the killing of Michael Brown, and in Brooklyn when Eric Garner was murdered. "And then," he says, "I was in the South for the first time as a black man traveling solo." But throughout the trip, Aryeh-Or tells me, he navigated race on the street by always being just outside the "normal cultural box" of what people were expecting. He'd wear a black leather jacket and broad-brimmed hat with a feather in it—"My rock star black ass with a Hollywood flair," he calls his style. "And then people would hear me speak!" His voice is sonorous, with an actor's clarity.

Just a few weeks into his trip, everything in Aryeh-Or's car was stolen. He posted on social media about the theft, and within a day someone he wrote for in front of Powell's Books in Portland offered him their typewriter as a gift to enable him to keep going.

Despite committing to spending a quarter of his year on the road, Aryeh-Or never considered committing to the lifestyle full-time. He scoffs a little at the idea of off-the-grid self-sufficiency as a goal. "Self-sufficiency is, by nature, arrogant," he says. "We put so much value on independence, but *inter*dependence is how we truly survive."

And though he knew he would return to a sedentary life, Aryeh-Or still found the transition jarring. "Coming back, you spend so much time in motion—and then suddenly you're still," he says. "As expected, not a fucking thing had changed. Only I was different.

"I got to experience how I show up when there's no backstory to me."

Something about being a stranger everywhere opened Aryeh-Or up. He took what he needed from the road and came home.

Curious to understand what it was like to be in one place again after committing to a life in motion, I call Paeton, Kevin's ex, who had traveled with him reading tarot on the road while he busked poetry. After their breakup, Paeton moved to Saint John in the Virgin Islands, a US territory east of Puerto Rico in the Caribbean. "The hardest part of the transition is finding a routine, which is hard to establish living in the van," Paeton tells me. She is a freckled, frizzy-haired woman in her midtwenties and had been in the van life for two and a half years. She tells me that it's only on the island, settled at last after years of travel around the country, that she's written her first poem.

"And you can't see it. It's very bad."

Paeton stopped street performing when she left her nomadic lifestyle. She said it felt like she was going too far down the rabbit hole of holding space for people reading tarot, giving so much of herself and taking on so much of other people's lives without support for her own mental health. Holding space meant being present to people's problems, a supportive shoulder as they worked them out. Sometimes people were in good places and she could laugh and play with them a little, sometimes they were at their most raw and vulnerable and needed a long conversation about suicide or substance abuse or family trauma. Tarot readers and typewriter poets alike have a maximum of about ten minutes to ascertain a person's needs and speak to them in a constructive way. It's emotional labor at a breakneck pace.

Being on the street also means being accessible to anyone, and people would also take Paeton's presence at her card table as an invitation not to buy her time for a reading but to flirt. Paeton doesn't just call what she does "busking," she calls it "lady busking." Women in public space are seen as fair game, Paeton says, and she quickly had to develop a sixth sense and a thick skin for predatory men. "When people would approach me, I'd have to take the power stance of the upper hand." She wore heavy makeup and eye glitter to be performative, and carried a concealed knife, though never had to use it. As her own boss, Paeton got good at moving people along. She didn't always have to be nice, she just had to be safe.

Besides the constant physical vigilance of the road, Paeton was taking on too many stories without a community to hold her stories. She pleased everyone by promising them a place in the universe, while denying herself the same thing. Without a steady income that didn't require massive amounts of emotional labor, she grew increasingly drained and fatigued.

Paeton traded her tarot cards for a service job at a café and bistro, where servility and politeness are job requirements. The shift she's having to make goes beyond her job. "One change settling down is that the things I say have more lasting repercussions, because we're all on this rock together," she says. "I'm so used to connecting deeply and then leaving the next week!" At under twenty square miles with a population of just over four thousand even before the hurricane exodus, Saint John is a small place after the expansiveness of the entire mainland US. It's a place where everyone knows everyone.

Saint John was attractive as a place removed from an old life that covered the mainland from coast to coast. An old friend from before Paeton's van life days, who was from Saint John, invited her to move out to the island and had a food service job lined up for her. As Paeton rebuilds herself from the breakup and discovers how to put down roots again, the island itself is rebuilding from the devastation of Hurricane Irma, the same hurricane that struck Puerto Rico in 2017. "You can't drink the water here," Paeton says, "the island is still recovering and the infrastructure is in disarray. Everything here is hard to do—so in that way, it's similar to living in a van." But, she tells me, after two months on the island, she finally moved her clothes from the suitcase that had held them for years into her closet.

Paeton is still trying to discover who she is without the partner, van, and lifestyle that were the cornerstones of her identity for years. "Apparently I've talked about the van every day I've been here," she confesses. "I still feel like a guest in the home I'm paying rent in." She got so used to being conscious of people's generosity every time she was in a house or taking a hot shower, but she's struggling to regain the feeling that she's entitled to these things. "In van life," she tells me, "the exchange value in relationships is laid bare—I always felt like what I was being given was so much larger than what I could give back, so I'd go the extra mile for people." She pauses. "I hope that part stays.

"I don't want to let go of the van life lifestyle," Paeton says, "but I don't know how wise it would be to try to maintain it by myself. Kevin and I would always talk about the curse of too much freedom, how being able to do anything makes it impossible to commit to doing anything, even with another person to bounce ideas off of."

Still, moving back into a house, with roommates, after living in the van with a partner also has its advantages. "I can let my guard down here," Paeton says, "there's a privacy you don't get in a van, where anyone can approach you at any time—a crazy person or a cop can always knock. Here I have more control of my environment."

Starting to put down roots means, for the first time, that other people leave the place Paeton's living before she does. "In February, a friend is moving," Paeton says, choking up. "For once, I'm going to be the person left behind. I haven't known that feeling." She remembers times in her travels when friends she made would try to convince her to stay in a given city and she'd brush them off—that wasn't her lifestyle.

"Every relationship I had for years had an end date," she says.

Jeremy, another van-dwelling typewriter poet, tells me he has no plans to go back to society. I catch up with him on his way to Rubber Tramp Rendezvous, a gathering in the Arizona desert of thousands of folks who have made the choice to live off the grid in vans, buses, RVs, and Airstream trailers. Many of these folks are old-timers who have been living this way for decades. The free meet-up is a chance to swap stories, exchange tips, and maybe just feel a little less alone on the road.

Jeremy is a trans man with a mop of curls on his head and a plaid shirt he wears half buttoned so his chest hair shows proudly from under a chunky stone pendant. He speaks about "society" in broad terms with just a touch of conspiracy theory thrown in, a sense that behind the expectations and norms of "the American dream" there's something planned and sinister, the theft of both autonomy and the community, what he calls van life's "tribal lifestyle."

Jeremy was in the middle of a road trip in the spring of 2015, one of his first experiments living out of his car, when he met an ex-girlfriend of Kevin's in Arizona, who told him he should try busking poems to fund his travel. Jeremy had always loved old things (he was an avid vinyl collector) and happened to be traveling with a typewriter to write letters to people. "I remember the first poem I ever wrote for a stranger," Jeremy says, "as I was on this trip to try to rediscover my purpose. Their topic was 'epiphany.'"

Jeremy grew up in a military family and was constantly moving around as a kid. He tried to settle down in his early adult life in Portland, Oregon, where he was married and lived in a house for eight years during his twenties until a divorce—he doesn't talk much about that. In his thirties, he tells me, "I'm no longer willing to hand over my soul and time, hustling for a place to put stuff I never get to enjoy because I'm too busy hustling.

"I actually bought the van I live in now from a guy I wrote a poem for on the street," he tells me. He's converted the red 1996 Ford E150 to have solar panels on top, hardwood paneling on the interior, adjustable colored lights, and both a bed space and small living space with a fridge, storage, and a long bookshelf. It looks incredibly sketchy parked out on the street between expensive cars on Fairfax, less so on my street in South Central when

I invite Jeremy over to use my stove to cook dinner. We first met over Instagram, and now he's stopping by on his way out to the desert for some R and R.

It was only after Jeremy discovered I was queer that he shared his gender history with me. (I write about it here with his consent.) He told me that van life and typewriter poetry had both "definitely gotten easier since my transition, with more opportunities and less getting moved along. Though I don't know if that's because of the privilege of people seeing me as a straight white guy, or if it's just because I've been doing it for longer and am better at it."

Part of the freedom of living in the van for Jeremy has been the option to work when work feels right and go boogie boarding with friends in the middle of the day if that feels better. "I live on the beach making under thirty thousand dollars a year." Jeremy smiles, telling me he's settled down in the last year predominantly in San Diego, which has less restrictive parking laws than many cities. For money, he busks typewriter poetry, sells magic stones and crystals, drives for Lyft (not out of the van but in his smaller car), and sells off his old record collection. As with Kevin, the freedom of work is a double-edged sword, and Jeremy cites being his own boss and self-motivation as the hardest parts of what he does.

"Part of van life is non-attachment," Jeremy says. In addition to getting rid of most of his stuff, he has a minute awareness of everything his body needs to consume and everything it gets rid of in a week. It's a shift in his relationship both with his body and with the earth itself, and he calls the process "de-alienation." On Instagram, his story fills the day after his visit with photos of him doing yoga, shirtless, in the desert.

Jeremy speaks lovingly about a typewriter poet in New York who only comes out to write in the subway when he feels depressed. "I aspire to be more like that poet. This practice is some sort of medicine," he says. I think about Paeton's exhaustion at having to hold space for people, the line between personal healing and healing someone else.

"The American dream has been dismantled and is being rewritten," Jeremy says. For him, "poetry is part of healing those wounds." Jeremy thinks about the work as a sort of trance channeling and he says that when he's writing it feels like it's not even really him. He's deeply invested in new age spirituality and talks about his life as an exercise in manifesting what he wants. He has become something of a historian of typewriter poets in his travels, making a point to meet and connect with people writing poems for strangers on typewriters in cities across the country. In many ways, I think, he sees me and other typewriter poets as fellow spiritual practitioners on the same path.

Jeremy keeps a catalog of all the typewriter poets he's met (there are dozens) and loves to talk about them. He says all have something of a wandering streak, even if they're not living in their vehicles. They are constantly treading ground around the country, around the world, to find moments for poetry in new places. He talks with me about putting together a typewriter poet convention or hosting some sort of formal gathering. But the players change constantly, and everyone is broke, and community beyond the occasional chance encounter or phone calls feels in some ways like a wistful fantasy, like a mirage on the horizon. We know it's a mirage, but we keep driving.

# The Dreamer

In 2016, leading up to the California primaries and the general election, after four years of full-time poetry, I ran a project called #poetsatthepolls. In LA, I convinced poets to blanket polling stations writing typewriter poetry for voters. We even got funding from a foundation trying to increase voter engagement through what they were calling "parties at the polls." The goal: to give voting the feeling of a capital-E Experience.

At the polls that day, people in LA were already celebrating what felt like a certain victory, though there was a deeper sense of unease that it might take more to make the country whole again with all the old wounds that had been reopened. The Young Republicans, sitting opposite my writing desk at an election watch party that had hired me, got drunker and rowdier as the evening wore on. "What would you like a poem about?" I asked one.

"Drain the swamp!" he replied.

I wrote him a piece on habitat destruction and native land rights.

The night Donald Trump was elected president, I wrote poems

as I watched the results come in and felt the energy of people
approaching my typewriter in liberal California wither. The top-
ics people gave me slid from hope into terror, from "breaking the
glass ceiling" to "learning to live together again." "Fake news" was
a topic on everyone's lips. It was like people didn't know what
story they were living in anymore.

Stepping back,
listen, the swirling chatter
of antagonism, 24/7 news
cycle, echo chambers of
re-tweets and after the
sound & fury this silence
creeping up on us will speak
volumes—how we break it—
will it be history breaking?
Democracy, civil society
itself coming apart at
the seams? What ceilings
we shatter and who stands
underneath them.

Catch a shard of rose glass
for your neighbor. Are they
building a mosaic? Can we
build a mosaic? From all
the broken pieces. Something

to look through, when it
gets too quiet or too loud.
Step back. No Rome. No ruin.

Since that fateful night, more women and women of color
started running for office than ever. Two years later I found myself
behind the typewriter at another election watch party in Chattanooga, Tennessee, in 2018. For the past week, I'd been trailing the
campaign of Melody Shekari for state house of representatives in
Tennessee as poet-in-residence, with unlimited access to the campaign and a mandate only to write. If nothing else good came from
the midterms, I thought I could at least try to find some poetry.

But prospects were bright. Progressive newcomers were expected to oust incumbents right and left in a Trump backlash during
these congressional elections. At Shekari's watch party, the crowd
that gathered held their breath for her, but also for the country.

Shekari was a first-generation Iranian American woman on
the verge of finding out if she would be the Democratic voice in
her state's congress for the fourth-largest city in Tennessee, and
her campaign mobilized a whole generation of young educated
progressive women in the South. One of them, a political science
master's student, asked for a poem about how every assignment
she was given in school ended up becoming a treatise on gender.
The student was here in formal wear, sitting next to her boyfriend.
Having spent a week with Melody, seeing firsthand the leering
she endured as a woman running for office, even from her men-
tors, this poem came easily:

How can every project not
evolve into an exposé
of underrepresentation
when every mirror
I've ever looked in
has been of my own making,
hard fought and only
sometimes won?

Bodies and politics
always fail
to be two different things
so I put my own on the line—
my body, my politics,
still knocking doors
as if to say, "still here."

If I keep showing up,
will you?

Rain or shine, win or lose
        loudly unafraid.

The student takes her poem with a polite smile and turns back to the TV. Perhaps I'm just misreading southern hospitality, but it seems like no one here wants to be seen celebrating too soon. What if they're on the losing team, again? In local races like this, there is no big data, so the results are up in the air until they are announced.

I look up from where I'm writing to see Melody, the woman of the hour, a pillar of calm putting her nervous supporters at ease. She wears her trademark blue campaigning dress and blazer, a light-skinned woman in her early thirties with a moon face and just a trace of adult acne showing through under the makeup. The crowd assembled reflects her—young, diverse, and college-educated, with lots of immigrants and children of immigrants: the new face of the South. Jen, Shekari's campaign manager, refreshes the screen every few seconds. Only Jen can see it, and she keeps a poker face while playing "I Will Survive" and Beyoncé's "Diva." Jen reports, precinct by precinct, as the results come in, and a crowd of young women and middle-aged Iranians gathers.

Shekari has been running for office in her hometown of Chattanooga, Tennessee, since she graduated from law school four years ago. She started with a long-shot national campaign for congress as a Democrat in a deep red state, and has been working on entrenching herself into the fabric of her community since then through volunteering and activism. This election is the result of almost six months of door knocking in every neighborhood, thousands of face-to-face conversations with constituents. "We've done everything we can do," she reminds her fidgety campaign staff for the whole week leading up to the primary, over and over, while I trail them. They know the state assembly race is tight, with five candidates in the field, but she's counting on the other candidates to split the vote and pave her a pathway to victory.

I knew Melody Shekari back when she was in law school at USC, or, as she calls them, "My ratchet days!" She was a different person then from the earnest-yet-polished politician she is walking a tightrope to become with this campaign, more relaxed, living up the last years of her college life. Since moving home, she had been trying to get me to come visit the South and make art with her community. The campaign was the perfect excuse—I would visit, write, and get an inside look into how a political campaign is its own sort of poetry.

Melody gets southern in her hospitality from the very first phone call we had to plan the trip. She won't hear of me booking my own shuttle from the Atlanta airport. She insists on taking care of it, even though she's in the middle of running for public office. And she tells me not to rent a car, that as long as I'm insured, I can use (and she uses the royal "we") "one of ours." It's clear, just from this call, that I'll be treated like family.

She's waiting for me when I arrive from the airport in a white car with a "Vote Melody Shekari" sticker plastered to one side. As she pulls up, one of the young women in my shuttle looks out the window at the waiting car and says, "Oh my god, I went to high school with her!" It's my first hint that Chattanooga is one of those places where everyone knows *everyone's* business.

Chattanooga is the doorway to the Deep South, the spot where cotton meets corn. During the Civil War, while most of

East Tennessee voted to remain part of the Union, its big city overwhelmingly voted to secede. The city became a Confederate stronghold and key strategic location until the Union took the city and began an uneasy occupation. In the decades that followed the war, northern leadership leaned on the black community's votes to keep political power in Chattanooga. This led to an unprecedented level of black involvement at various levels of municipal government before Jim Crow laws were passed in the late nineteenth century to silence the community once again.

Melody is running, she tells me, in a district that's been gerrymandered to be overwhelmingly black. This means it almost always elects a Democrat, but also that it's systematically disenfranchised in the numbers game as one of two staunchly Democratic districts versus seven that always vote Republican. Both sides have embraced gerrymandering, Melody sighs, to consolidate their constituents and ensure safe seats. But in exchange for a few easy races, the Democrats have given up ever winning a majority.

Melody takes me on her own tour of Chattanooga-at-night from the moment I arrive. We don't need light to see the Chattanooga she knows, a data dump she streams directly into my brain of council district lines, average income brackets, and racial demographics.

In contrast, when I'd made small talk with people on the airplane shuttle about the places we were driving through, the woman next to me had been eager to point out sites of historical battles, her mental maps divided by bloodshed. "Why is it called 'The Volunteer State'?" I ask her, only to be answered by the twangy youth sitting behind me: "War of 1812," he said, and nothing more, and everyone nodded like that should clear all my questions up.

Tennessee has ten days of early voting, and the first place I go with Melody is an early voting site, where she's going to visit her dad before a day of events and door knocking. Her dad has been holding down the fort in the scorching sun and humidity day after day, she tells me. He's a tiny powerhouse in his sixties, with weathered arms and a face that splits open with his grin as he waves at people driving into the polls, screaming "Vote for Melody!" at their sealed car windows. He gets called "Campaign Dave" and "Campaign Dad" indiscriminately during my stay. And he takes his job very—very—seriously. "If it were up to him," Melody tells me, "we'd all be at the polls every day.

"But he lives in an information-poor world," Melody says, flicking through her iPhone. Her world is a constant stream of information, and she checks by the minute on how many impressions Facebook analytics say her latest post has, always evaluating the heaps of cash she's pouring into her online presence. This is her campaign strategy—her opponents have the old guard and the black church vote locked down, but she has social media savvy and is confident that she can out-saturate them in the information landscape. In a world of local elections, where no one beyond the elected officials is really aware of the political battles that play out around policy, name recognition could be enough. Melody's run is banking on it.

After long days campaigning, Melody takes me downtown to a few hipster bars to unwind, but she can't escape campaign work. From the moment we enter, she starts working her way through the crowd of young professionals and southern socialites, exchanging pleasantries with people she knew in high school and making sure everyone sees her face and knows voting is happening Thursday and that she will personally drive all of them to the polls if they ask. She makes this promise to, it seems, literally everyone, and I start to wonder if on election day we'll wind up transforming into a full-time taxi service.

It's only back at Melody's place after the bar, settling into our laptops on the couch, that she is able to tap into a network of people beyond this little bubble to get some relief from the pressure cooker of the campaign. Melody is on social media to connect with voters, but also to escape them. Everyone in Chattanooga just wants to talk about the elections, but beyond that network no one online cares about Melody's race. For a brief moment scrolling through friends' vacation photos she can pretend it isn't consuming her every waking thought.

"That's why I'm glad you're here," Melody tells me. "You, at least, have some distance and perspective."

Melody says she still keeps in touch with lots of friends from law school in different areas of the country, but she also shares that she taps into these networks regularly for fundraising, and between scrolling through photos she checks her analytics one more time, for good measure, out of anxiety or just chasing that jolt of dopamine.

The average household income in Chattanooga is twenty-five thousand dollars, right at the poverty line for a family of four, but the city is experiencing the seventh-highest rate of rent inflation in the US. This inflation means all the work the city council has done to attract tech and incentivize artists is working—but at the expense of people who are priced out of their homes, who literally lose their status as part of the community when they are forced to move away. In a system of politics where representation is based on home address, bringing economic development can itself be a way of silencing part of the population by forcing those without means to move.

Melody says that, if she wins, she'll be the first nonreligious candidate from this district. She's positioned herself as the LGBT+ ally candidate, in a landscape where the church doesn't abide gayness, and there's no separation between church and civic leaders. We go to a city council meeting presentation with gay and trans activists, and Melody offers her own pocketbook to pay for them to get their message out. If Melody's competitors have their church congregations, I think, she has the gay vote and the yuppie bar crowd—but coming from LA, I know these groups as the much-touted harbingers of gentrification.

As the election draws nearer, Campaign Dave, an Iranian immigrant, keeps saying to himself, "She has the white vote!"

"You can't say that, Dave!" Melody tells him. She always calls her father by his first name. She is aware of the politics going on here—but she also wants to win. In the final days before the election, Melody bites the bullet and hires paid door knockers, a crew of older black men who were recommended by a political mentor. "You know I'm already getting calls," the organizer says, "calling me traitor." The word *race* is unspoken but implied. I wonder how much things have changed since the old days of buying votes, as we zoom away from the housing projects these paid canvassers will cover.

Though she grew up in this town, Melody tells me she always felt like an outsider as a kid. "I got a lot of hate growing up from my classmates because I was Persian, especially after 9/11," she says. "Up until recently, I never claimed where I was from." In many ways, this election is Melody trying to reimagine her relationship with the town where she grew up, beyond black and white. If the prodigal daughter of Muslim immigrants could come back and win the people's trust, win the right to represent them, then maybe some of that history of hate could be redeemed.

I split my time between campaigning and writing in the public library, which sets up a table for me next to the League of Women Voters. People tell me about love and family and friends and uncertainty, but also a lot about God. One of the librarians tells me her word is "Jesus!" When I pry her for more information, she tells me about the educational programs she runs for kids, but really for Jesus. I write her:

I save my praise for Him
   in a simple box, unadorned
     with ornament. Open my palms
        to let what will speak
through me speak—
in crowded classrooms,
to kids who've been given
    up on once too often,
I offer words, sustain
        myself on The Word,
            see His hands
      in every everyday miracle
of language passing
      children's lips.

I'm sure there are higher
callings. But this is mine.
An unshirking duty, light
to ignite all the little
   fires until the whole city
    is aglow. And none of this
is for me & none of this
   is for me & all of this
        is His.

During children's hour at the library, I take my typewriter
into the kids' room and invite them to play on it. There are just

two sisters in the room when I get there, ages seven and ten, and the older keeps cartwheeling. She breaks from her cartwheeling to write a wartime letter like something I imagine she'd have seen in history books: "Dear family, I miss you and hope to see you soon . . ."

The younger girl writes what she tells me is a song. "It's about being misunderstood and being an orphan," she says while her mom sits watching.

The mom's shirt, from the YMCA, says, "CONNECT: verb / ke-nect / to link or join, bring together, bind together (as in a community)." With each new person I talk to, there's a clear tension in the New South in how people are trying to connect, to bind together, beyond historical and all too contemporary divisions. Creating imaginary lines and solidifying them into reality, into solidarity. Melody tells me endorsements have come privately, but all the politicians are hedging their bets publicly, while adding each other on social media, just in case.

Weirdly, though Melody introduces me to everyone as "a poet from LA," no one bats an eye or asks follow-up questions. At the library, people are appreciative but almost unsurprised to find me there. They ask for their poems seriously, thoughtfully, trusting me with the intimate details of their lives, from secrets to divorces, as though having a poet write for them is an everyday occurrence. Compared to the exclamations of surprise at finding a poet that I'm used to on the coasts or in the Midwest, the South plays its hand close to its chest.

— — —

When I'm not writing, most of my time volunteering for the campaign is spent door knocking. Melody has been personally knocking on doors for months, covering huge swaths of the district where, she says proudly, "we know our competition hasn't even been." The first neighborhood we visit is anchored by a Taco Bell, a few pawnshops, a hospice, and a Baptist church all sharing the same corner. The houses here all have broad lawns and lots of dogs, with old cars stacked up in the driveways. Gas grills sit out front, waiting for the weekend, and the streets are lined with big magnolia trees and creeping vines. Mosquitoes eat us alive as we walk and pass out flyers. Cicadas make a low hum as the sun streaks clouds to turn the whole sky yellow. Campaign Dave notes that all the houses have small windows and all the curtains are drawn, though it's not yet dark out.

We come to a house with two black guys in their early thirties sitting out front on a pickup, shooting the shit and drinking Bud Lights. No one raises an eyebrow at bringing us into their conversation, as though we'd known each other for years. One is a musician, and to my surprise the thing he wants Melody to take back to the state capital is the need for after-school music programs. "People complain about the gangs, but the kids don't have anything to do," he tells us. He's worked with lots of famous hip-hop artists (he shows me on his phone) and has a tattoo of the letters PGM. When I ask what they mean, he says, "Paid Get Money." Art and commerce, commerce and art.

"What do you think of athletes kneeling at the national anthem?" the musician asks. It's not something a state-level politician can affect, but it's a litmus test for Melody, who in this crowd of black folks is looking distinctly pale.

I want to get out my typewriter and write for these guys, to get to know them, but Melody can only stay with each household for so long. She is trying to knock on every door, even if it means cutting off conversations. There just isn't time. Reluctantly I climb back into the SUV.

Next we find an old white man with a white beard and yellow teeth, welding in his driveway. We shout for his attention over the sound of power tools, but he doesn't notice us. His tabby cat, with a stub tail, slides off his car as we approach and comes for a scratch. As we get closer, we see the car is covered in rude stickers slamming Trump, which give the impression that he's designed them himself. One prominent bumper sticker features a bad photoshop of Trump and Putin holding each other as gay leather daddies.

When the old guy finally pauses in his welding, he jumps up, excited to see us. Melody tries to tell him about what she hopes to do for the neighborhood, but no matter what she brings up, the conversation inevitably flips to the national news. He starts with Trump but then goes back to Bush versus Gore before spinning sideways into recapping early Stephen Colbert and then political sketches on *SNL* in the 1970s. She wants to talk about politics. This is what politics means, to him.

"I hope we can count on your vote!" Melody calls out, waving as we beat a hasty retreat to the car. She marks a "yes" vote on her door knocking app as we climb back in, though she didn't have a chance to get a word in edgewise.

Unless people are outside, no one opens their doors all the way, as if they are always a bit suspicious. All the houses in this neighborhood have metal plaques above their address numbers next to the door with images of geese or rabbits or dogs that watch our approach, silent as gargoyles. The final person we talk to that night is an old state patrol officer sitting on his porch. He has lived in his house in this neighborhood for fifty-six years. "Now the blacks have started taking over," he says, gesturing at the residential hillside sloping down from the house, "and you can't control them." He laughs. "And then I've got this illness," he tells us, "that no doctor can diagnose."

Campaign Dave starts to compare maladies and home remedies, until Melody drags him away. At the end of the day, the sixty-three-year-old man has so much energy after door knocking until 9 P.M. that he's shimmying along to "Last Dance" in the car on the way home. Melody and I are both exhausted.

Between relentless door knocking and car shouting at the polls, Campaign Dave spends his time sipping coconut water for his throat and coming up with new, unsolicited, campaign slogans. When we get to Melody's house, he prints out a new campaign sign that he's clearly made himself, with all the graphic design skills of a sixty-three-year-old. The sign says:

unity

diversity

integrity

shekari

. . . in big Times New Roman text with fun colors, and Campaign Dave keeps repeating the words to himself, delighting in the rhyme. Melody vetoes the homemade signs right away. It's four days before the election, and her dad is still making his own fanboy art, still perfecting campaign slogans to tell people as he door knocks. "Vote Melody Shekari for unity, diversity, integrity!" he tells people. "I should know, I raised her!"

Back home, hearing him try out this slogan, Melody's mother, Farah, arches an eyebrow and asks no one in particular, "Who raised her?"

The home Melody shares with her parents (she keeps this part quiet while campaigning) is nestled in a rapidly gentrifying area of Chattanooga, with rows of abandoned industrial and warehouse buildings being repurposed as redbrick cheese shops, art galleries, artisanal coffee roasters, and mindfulness centers. As we enter her house, Melody apologizes, saying, "It totally looks like Persia threw up in here!" If she hadn't mentioned it, I might not have noticed the little touches in an otherwise very cookie-cutter suburban American home—the decorative placemats, a traditional Persian painting above the shag-carpeted staircase.

Melody settles in over a spreadsheet for late-night financials that she has to send in to the state tonight. She's outraised all of her competition and is gleeful at her competence in the face of the other candidates, one of whom hasn't even filed and already owes the state thousands of dollars in late fees. "He's self-financing too," Melody tells me, with a wince that fails to hide a tinge of schadenfreude.

Campaign Dave migrates restlessly up and down the stairs, from us to his computer, talking joyously about a new job he's starting and is filling out his paperwork for. He's a nuclear engineer, and after being unemployed for a while he's been hired out of state. "That's it, I'm running away!" he tells Melody.

"The thing about Persian parents is that they love you so much they never want you to leave!" Melody says dryly. Both Farah and Campaign Dave beam at us, brimming over with pride and helpfulness, whether it's wanted or not.

The next morning, we rise early to take part in a final push for early voting, the March to the Polls. The march starts in the parking lot of a big Baptist church. Melody and her parents and I join around fifty parishioners and other candidates. "Winning isn't everything, it's the only thing!" Campaign Dave effuses, a mantra he's heard somewhere and repeats over and over.

"Yeah," Melody says, sarcastically, "I'm doing all this, but I don't really wanna win . . ."

"I'm gonna bite you three times after the election," her dad says.

"I was thinking about taking you on a last-minute trip, Dave," Melody says. "If your attitude improves, maybe I will!"

Two of the other candidates Melody is running against are here, and they keep a cold distance between them. Melody had gone to pull weeds in her blue campaign dress the day before the March to the Polls, clearing the underbrush that's covered up the graves in an all-but-forgotten African American cemetery. Her opponents accused her, online, of not really working. They suggested that she just used the cleanup for a photo op, because she was in a dress. A dress, for them, was not working attire.

A community leader we talk to, a proud black woman with a long history of activism, shudders at the thought of clearing the cemetery, bare legs or no. She says, "There's snakes out there! No way." Her voice changes on the word *snakes*, and I am reminded that we are in the parking lot of a Baptist church. Eve and the Fall are never far away.

Melody schmoozes and shakes hands with everyone, though most of these church folk are here in T-shirts emblazoned with other candidates' names. She won't win these people now, but showing up will be a start to get their vote in the general election against the Republican candidate if she can win her primary. She's in this for the long game.

One of the sitting county commissioners starts off the speeches once everyone has arrived, slipping easily into the cadence of a preacher and the language of the church. "Voting is part of fellowship," he tells us. A pastor brings us together for prayer before we walk, and we all join sweaty hands in the parking lot. The humidity has to be pushing 90 percent. "Lord, we ask you to add supernatural votes to the votes we cast." The pastor goes on to preach how Moses led his people out of bondage, as we sweat into one another's palms. The voice of the community is a divine mandate, he tells us.

He's the pastor of a church that meets in a converted Kmart, Melody tells me later. The parishioners number in the thousands. Melody, the daughter of Muslim immigrants, has her politician's smile on through all the fiery church rhetoric. Her moment comes after—as the crowd moves toward the polls, she whips out her phone to capture the whole thing on Facebook Live. Suddenly, she becomes popular. Everyone wants to talk to her on camera.

When the March to the Polls ends, so does early voting. Jen, the campaign manager, says that the only thing to do between now and Thursday, election day, is to get people out to vote. The numbers from early voting are already impressive—twenty thousand people voted early, and these primaries historically only see about a total of thirty thousand people voting. Freed from his position at the polls, Melody's dad paces the house, tallying the possibilities in his mind. He's a man who can't sit still.

On the evening before the election, I head up to the room I'm staying in while Melody lies on the couch, wide awake. When I arrived she showed me the room as "my room" with such confidence that it wasn't until halfway through the trip that I realized this wasn't a guest room, this was Melody's room, and she was spending the final week of her campaign for state office sleeping on her parents' couch. The sheer loneliness of it strikes me. Even when we were out in social spaces, Melody couldn't stop campaigning. On a local radio show, trying to appear personable, she insisted, "I have jokes!" And while we'd been cycling nonstop through other people's campaign events, Melody never hosts her own. "They're a waste of time for outreach," she tells me. "You only reach the people who already support you." As we wrap up our final phone banking the day before the election, we find we have not much to say to one another. Melody is too deep in the nervous echo chamber of her own mind.

There's not much of a tribe beyond her parents and campaign manager buoying Melody. She complains to me about how all relationships have become transactional, tit for tat, I'll scratch your back if you scratch mine. She's worried about dating prospects in office—how will she tell when she finds someone who wants to be close to her for her rather than for the office? Will there be a difference? She is attempting to eliminate herself as an individual in this running, to become an avatar of public will, an expression of collective power. It's what she wants more than anything. But she's also afraid.

Melody has other women running for office coming to her, now that she is running her second campaign, for advice. "I should write an article on how to dress as a woman running for office!" she tells me. "Seriously, no one teaches you these things. How to look professional and attractive so people will talk to you but not hit on you too hard. I've gained weight during the campaign and that helps. Afterward I may try to lose it again, but it acts as a sort of armor against the worst harassment."

I've been glued to Melody at the hip for the past five days, and I worry out loud that I am overstaying my welcome. Melody tells me not to worry about it. Growing up her family always had family members stay for months at a time as they emigrated from Iran to get on their feet. My week is nothing, she assures me from the couch she's sleeping on because she has literally given me her bed.

Melody's campaign manager signed me up as a poll watcher, so I go to the poll at the Redemption Church gym—a basketball court with green awnings and folded bleachers emblazoned with giant crosses and the letter *R* for *Redemption*. I chat with the poll workers, all of whom are here from the same Baptist church. Even at the polling place, religion spills into politics.

I sit in the gazebo in the park opposite the center for a long time, with my typewriter. In LA, at the polls, I was confident in belonging. Here, the stream of folks heading in remind me that I am an outsider, unsanctioned in this space. Melody's blessing is the blessing of a candidate, and therefore verboten on this hallowed ground. Instead of bringing out the typewriter and trying to set up outside, I sit inside with the closed case next to me. I write in my notebook, processing the proceedings for no one but myself as the world of the primary flows around me:

Steps echo
across the church gym
toward the flimsy tables with cardboard dividers,
    emblazoned with the word
VOTE.

A criss-crossed crossword—
which functions to which institution?
Ancient black women
practicing enfranchisement
as a sacred right, not taken for granted.

One drops her cane as she sits.
Her son picks it up.

The boy who left his raincoat
is not here to vote, he is looking
for his raincoat, he left it here yesterday.
"A raincoat?" "Yes, ma'am."
"You left it here yesterday?" "Yes, ma'am."
His shirt had a picture of a coiled snake.
"Defending Our Liberty" it says, and above that, "NRA."

Polls are open 8am–8pm.
Halfway through, the 80-year-old poll worker asks for coffee.
"I'm cold!" she says. Her fingers
trace precinct lines in addresses
down the page. This is a state
where you have to show a photo ID.

"This is why people don't vote!"
the young white guy says to no one,
filling out his address change paperwork.

"I just curbed the tire on my brand new car," he exclaims
in reply to a poll worker's, "How are you?"
"And it's my birthday!"
His chinos are wet.

The tablet has frozen, so the poll worker gets out
    the book of addresses
split into Streets and Courts and Avenues
so it's impossible to find anything quickly.
"It's two-thousand eighteen," the birthday boy says, pacing.
"Why do I still have to come some*place* to vote?"
His chinos squeak on the basketball gym floor,
thumbs flailing against a screen.
That, at least, will respond to his pleas.
"Ya'll are seeing it, we're living in a joke!"
he says, chewing discontent
into his cheeks.

A huge anxiety around physical place is built into this whole institution of voting. Who are we? Where do we live? Where are we from? In an age of perpetual displacement and transformation, these questions are terrifying because they are increasingly irrelevant. Despite public investment in high-speed wireless through fiber-optic cables and tax breaks to attract the first Volkswagen plant in decades, many of the older folks I talk to in Chattanooga are job insecure. Their skills have been outpaced by a new era of business, and they are either actively looking for work elsewhere or worried about layoffs as they train people in India to do their jobs. If people move every two years for work, or work with people halfway around the world online, what can it even mean to be in a community anymore?

In a way, Melody's campaign is a referendum on this placed placelessness in local politics. She is the Google AdWords candidate, the Facebook ads candidate, to the tune of $150 per day for the last couple days. While the others are in churches, Melody is online, hoping the younger voters she can reach this way will actually turn out, or that enough older folks have embraced Facebook.

And people on Facebook just want to know, "Do you support the wall?"

"They don't even live in the district!" Melody sighs. In this era, she can't help being caught up in national debates, even if they have nothing to do with the job she's running to do. All the TVs play Fox on silent, with computer generated subtitles filled with nonsensical transliterations of Trump's already garbled speeches. It becomes clear to me why he succeeded, like Obama before him, on the campaign trail. Both men became iconic in different ways, to the point where the handshake was more than a handshake, it was an affirmation of values and identity through the mere fact of presence. Like successful poets, successful candidates must be a mirror—people see the selves they want to be, whether that's a shrewd businessperson or an eloquent dreamer. At the end of the day, everybody just wants to see themselves.

So the people on Facebook asking Melody about the wall are trying to figure out if they see themselves in her. The local election is caught in the space between personal connection (like what I do writing poems) and icon handshake status—the whole point of field ops is to lay out the story for a candidate to fall into. Melody has done some of this herself by having run before state-wide and gained a party endorsement, but this is also a key part her dad plays—as her biggest booster and public cheerleader, he's creating a mythos—the hardworking immigrant, the good daughter, the close-knit new Tennessee family.

The day of the election, Melody posts a picture of a cracked shoe from all the walking she's done knocking on doors. "Where my family is from, women aren't allowed to run for office," she posts, delicately avoiding the word *Iran*.

Melody's parents bicker, as all couples do—"You chose me," Dave tells Farah, at one point, after being reprimanded for something.

"I didn't choose you, my family did," Farah says, equal parts snide and loving, and I realize that, decades back, this picturesque suburban couple must have had an arranged marriage.

For all Melody is from here, she can never really be from here, I think. Her parents are excited to take me out to Cracker Barrel, to celebrate the Americanness they have won through a lifetime of work. But for their daughter, who is neither white nor black, neither immigrant nor old blood, this election is about more than power. It's about belonging.

— — —

But the pull of history is strong.

When the results came in, Melody placed second, ahead of three other candidates but still thousands of votes behind Youssef, an older black man with a scandal-laden political career who she wrote off because he was recently forced out of the city council in disgrace. She had to rise to make a speech to her assembled family and fans at the watch party once the results became clear. "The best candidate doesn't always win," she says. "We saw that in 2016. But that doesn't mean we can stop trying."

In private, she has another story.

"This is what losing feels like," Melody tells her campaign manager, Jen, bitterly. Jen, who wears the semicolon tattoo of attempted suicide, survived, proudly on her right wrist. When I wrote her a poem, her theme was "overcoming adversity."

The next morning, I go outside to find that someone, I assume Campaign Dave, has already taken the campaign stickers off the car. It's plain white now, just another anonymous car on a street of anonymous cars belonging to private anonymous citizens just going about their lives in suburban Tennessee. Melody doesn't get out of her pajamas that day, though there's still a string of pearls around her neck. She looks different, and I realize it's the first time I've seen her without makeup this whole trip.

The morning is deathly quiet. "Dave is being an asshole," Melody tells me. "He doesn't know how to mourn." She rises only to help her mother cook, a small, shared ritual that can be done in silence. There's a strength in these two women's camaraderie.

Melody tells me she doesn't want to leave the house, anticipating the well wishes and sympathy that will inevitably follow her because she knows everyone in this town. Today she just wants to be sad, without meeting anyone's expectations.

"I'm breaking up with an idea today," Melody says. She laughs as I reach for my notes to write the sentence down. "Brian, I knew you'd like that! That one's for you!" Her voice is not sarcastic or bitter. It's drained but loving. This is what she wanted. Someone to witness her effort, rise or fall. Someone from the outside to remind her that the world is bigger, that there are other paths still stranger than hers to fulfillment.

Before I leave Chattanooga, Melody and I climb a mountain. You can't see the city from this lookout, just the valley on the other side. The mountainside is a lush green, rocks jutting out from what Melody tells me are kudzu vines, an invasive species that farmers brought to steady the soil, but that now chokes out the native trees where they stand.

Grief is a funny thing. A mourning for a future whose possibility has ended. We drive through the kudzu mountainside in complete silence. Mel knows every turn to get up this mountain without a map—she was once the high schoolers we find at the top. They chat about family and school, about what's next. This is the end of summer, and everyone is gearing up for new semesters, new chapters of life.

Once on the mountain I am itching to explore, but Melody is still hurting too much. While I bound down the trail past rock climbers, relieved to be out of the house, she sits on a stone look-ing out over the cliff, the native daughter of Tennessee reading *Native Son*. Still trying to inhabit blackness, I think, to connect with blackness and better serve the constituents who have told her, however sincere her efforts, that she cannot represent them.

Scrambling down the hill, I come on an empty field inhabited only by Civil War statues. I stop to try to read the plaques under-neath each statue, to try to understand the history, but the parade of names belongs to another world, a deep history that trusts you already know each battle's importance and the allegiances of each regiment. I can't even tell which side the statues were fighting for, most of the time. No one will make statues of Melody, or her op-ponent, I think. We are past that time in history. Our sculptures now are postmodern, shapes and colors, clean lines free of messy history.

"I feel like a ghost here," Melody tells me over the phone two months later. I remember the line of the Christian librarian's poem: "and none of this is for me." What does it mean to offer yourself as a politician, an embodiment of the public will? Do you find your authentic story or lose yourself so you can reflect everyone?

And what does it mean, then, for the public to pass you over? For your friends and neighbors and strangers you thought you knew to say, "There are better mirrors."

How can you know yourself when the mirror shatters?

I arrive back from my wanderings in time to watch the sun set with Melody, on my last evening in Tennessee. She is still without words, will be without words or direction in life for a long time. But this evening on the mountainside, as the sun sets, she still has the capacity to snap a selfie commemorating my visit. Phone in hand, facing the empty valley, facing the dusk, facing all of Facebook, the day after losing her election, she digs deep to bring out her best politician's smile.

# Self-Proclaimed
# Witches and
# Deviants

## I.

It's an oppressively humid midsummer in New England, and I'm sitting in a darkened theater with a cross section of Massachusetts tourists in too-low cargo shorts and literal red socks. Around the walls are mannequins, frozen forever in the drama of the 1600s witch trials. I stare up into the face of the devil. He is bolted high up on the wall, with his eyes glowing red.

"There *never* were witches in Salem," a voice crackles from the speakers.

Satan looks like he's from a B-horror movie, a long-fingered diorama in red light. I was expecting animatronics, but the show we've paid to see is just mannequins and spotlights as a recording plays. The narration muses on whether the supernatural exists or if it's only human superstition. The lights go down on the devil and up on a procession of puritan women in frocks and bonnets gathered around beds, then silhouetted as an angry mob. The mannequins are dusty with the occasional cobweb stretching from a finger catching the light. Nothing looks like it's been touched since the 1980s.

The recorded voice sounds suspiciously gleeful in describing the grisly torture and execution of innocent person after innocent person. This is the exciting part of the story. The assembled congregation of tourists shifts in their seats to see the dioramas of the jail, the man on the gallows, and the man being crushed to confession under the rocks, confessing nothing, only challenging his captors to add more weight. "More weight!" the recorded narration intones, in the spooky tones of a ghost story.

Then, as the diorama light show ends, the narrator sweeps all the spooky suspense away with a few lines. Of course, the voice tells us, there never were witches in Salem. The trials were the result of rampant paranoia on the part of "hysterical girls." Nothing supernatural to see here, just a bit of 1980s museum sexism. The next room hammers home the New England message of rationality and pluralism, sweeping the rug out from under the feet of the gleeful ghosts. Yet another set of dioramas draws a historical narrative of witchcraft from pre-Christian midwives to a pair of Wiccans, male and female, who assure us with tinny audio that they are a legitimate religious group with no claims to magical power. Because, of course, the museum makes it very clear, magic isn't real.

As we exit through the expansive gift shop, the woman who brought me here grins under her pointed hat. "There never were witches in Salem?" she repeats and raises an eyebrow. "You can't walk down the street here without tripping on one!"

It's Holy Crow, the palm reader from Electric Forest a year and a half ago.

And she says she can control the weather.

Holy Crow's given name is Eowyn, and I visit her and her partner, Meff, in Salem. They are gearing up for October, or as they call it, "spooky season." This is their Black Friday and Christmas all rolled into one. The witches pick me up from the airport in Boston in their little beat-up Toyota, which gradually falls apart over the course of my visit. Eowyn wears a high-brimmed felt hat with a witchy peak, and a vest covered with patches. The biggest one, prominent dead-center on the back, says: "Ain't afraid of no ghosts or fascists." Next to that, another reads: "Queer as in fuck you."

Eowyn (yes, named after the Lord of the Rings character) and I have worked a number of events together around the country since Electric Forest—me as a poet, her as a witch. She outearns me by hundreds of dollars every time, selling amulets and jewelry and reading palms. Her partner, Meff, uses they/them/their pronouns and made a living working in tech for decades. But for the past two years, since Meff lost their job, the couple has been relying on the income from Holy Crow, which like RENT Poet is both Eowyn's pseudonym and business entity. I'm here to see how they make the magic happen (pun gleefully intended) and to get to the bottom of a small start-up selling the only product that seems more immaterial than poetry: magic.

At the end of my first month writing poems full-time as a typewriter poet on the street, I wrote a reflection: "I find that the writing is like a spell—something people ask for to change themselves. Elsewhere, they would go to a fortune-teller, a shaman: 'I need a potion!' 'I only sell poems, will that do?'" I had started soliciting people by saying, "Do you *need* a poem? Not want, need."

So now I'm on a pilgrimage to this woman who sells spells and makes no bones about it. I always struggle in my work thinking about poetry and value, to believe that my words can be what someone needs to hear, and therefore be worth something.

My parents were hardcore atheists and rationalists, but I grew up in the heart of new age LA thinking where "What's your sign?" was often the second piece of information people wanted to know after your name. I'd always rolled my eyes at this. But as a queer kid finding my way, I did often find that the categories people commonly used to position each other—married? kids? family?—didn't apply to people in my community. There was a sense that this natural order was not natural to us, that it did not serve us.

In an era of infinite unverifiable online information, conspiracy theories, and fake news, the promise of literal "magic" is enjoying a comeback. The millennials at the heart of this revival of magical thinking care less about whether the tools they are using are real than whether they are *useful*. On the hunt for an academic grounding to explain this craving for make-believe, I find the work of Harvard human evolutionary biology professor Joseph Henrich. He speculates that divination rituals act as crude randomizing devices that help people overcome their natural decision-making biases, in situations where those biases would lead to people making worse decisions than random chance.

Magic, the research posits, can counter people's inability to act in the face of an uncertain and stressful future with overwhelming quantities of data. When you don't know where to turn—leave it up to chance!

But chance in magical practices is delivered in the most human way imaginable—in the form of a story. The promise of fortune-telling is not that the recipient will hear the truth, but that whatever the fortune-teller reads has the potential of being what that person *needs* to hear. I think of the preface to John Green's novel *The Fault in Our Stars*, which is partly based on a true story, in which he says, "Neither novels nor their readers benefit from attempts to divine whether any facts hide inside a story." And then, rather snarkily, he goes on to enlist the reader's necessary complicity: "I appreciate your cooperation in this matter."

Was all magic just, as I suspected, wacky stories and people's own confirmation bias? Yes and no, the research seemed to suggest. None of it was real, but it was all *real*. As real as people choose to make any story.

"Witchcraft is in a renaissance since the Harry Potter generation hit adulthood," Eowyn tells me. We trek around downtown Salem, which is just a couple streets, packed with magic shops. We go into a wand shop with signs up disclaiming that, though they sell Harry Potter branded merchandise, they are not affiliated with

Warner Bros. or the franchise. There *is* a sanctioned Harry Potter store next door, though, and, just next to it, the oldest witchcraft shop in the country.

Outside the old shop, someone has written what look like Norse runes in pink and blue chalk on the sidewalk. Inside, it looks much the same as the other witchy stores. Tables lined with herbs in individual-size packets, touting their properties. Candles labeled by what burning them will provide. The themes are disconcertingly similar to what people ask me to write them poems about: courage, gratitude, confidence, love.

"Look, rope magic!" Eowyn says, and I turn to see strings of hanging rope, knotted around cards, gemstones, and handwritten blessings with burnt edges. In each witch shop, Eowyn points out an herb or a candle to tell me what it's for. The shopkeepers join in, and soon they are having a lively discussion about the use of various stones, cards, teas, and trinkets in different traditions. Everything is referenced, and Eowyn's references almost always go deeper than the shopkeepers'. She's all about her research.

I nod at the list of magical properties and roll my eyes a bit internally.

As we come out, we have to shout to be heard over the sound of construction. Salem is booming, and they are rebuilding a facade opposite the magic shops. "Fifteen years ago, when I moved here, it was dead," Eowyn tells me. "It's just recently that it's been consciously transformed into an international tourist destination. Living in Salem is like moving into an office park for me."

— — —

Massachusetts is in the middle of a heat wave, and all Eowyn wants to do the day I arrive is head down to the beach. It's a small cove with a rocky bottom where the river meets the ocean, and we change and jump into the water, delighting in the cold. The witches have picked up what turn out to be wine coolers, and we toast my arrival in the Atlantic, a little welcome ceremony.

Meff and Eowyn splash around together, their love palpable. Eowyn calls Meff "monkey" and kisses them, while an overweight man watches disapprovingly from the shoreline. After a few more minutes, we get out. Walking back, they say, "It was time for us to leave," and comment on the threat they observed in the watching man's body language when they showed physical affection, an ever-present danger for folks beyond the gender binary in public spaces.

During my stay in Massachusetts, the state puts a referendum on the ballot asking the public if they want to scrap the protections for trans and nonbinary people that the legislature has put in place. Meff is from Boston, but Eowyn is from the South originally and says she hasn't been back to her hometown in North Carolina for two years, since the state passed discriminatory anti-trans bathroom bills. She refuses to go back to a place that discriminates against her partner.

Salem has strict busking laws, designed, Eowyn says, to deter Christian protestors who come to speak out against witchcraft, so I can't take my typewriter out into the town to busk poetry. This is the way I usually get to know a place, so I feel a little blind here. Fortunately, Eowyn's house is a revolving door of humans, who come to talk marketing strategy, eat, give tattoos, exchange gossip about who's doing what in the community, and paint their nails. Eowyn is in the process of building the WitchPunx Collective and calls its members WitchPunx—"With an *X*!" she exclaims. I recognize the linguistic strategy of using an *X* at the end of a word to de-gender it from Spanish, where "Latino" and "Latina" get shorthanded to "Latinx" to make a gendered language more inclusive. The WitchPunx are all young nonbinary people, who Eowyn is mentoring in both life and witchcraft.

A new WitchPunx member named Saul, who has agreed to take on social media for the collective, comes over on a sweltering afternoon. Ostensibly they are there to talk media strategy and vending, but mostly, as I sense happens a lot with this work, they talk about life. For young queers charting their own outsider paths, Eowyn and Meff are the rare example of a strong, nonbinary couple in their thirties. They are de facto parents, and of course they feed everyone, taking special care to accommodate dietary restrictions. Eowyn calls the collective "my kids."

Saul wears thick gauge earrings, a lip stud between the nose and mouth, and cut-off jeans with a matching jean jacket emblazoned with a lapel pin that says, "they/them/theirs." They were raised Irish Catholic, with Republican parents, and like most of their peers in the 2000s, they first found and were drawn to what they call "pagan wiccanism" online.

"I identify as trans masc nonbinary," Saul says. *Trans* comes from the Latin, "across," on the other side of, while *masc* is shorthand for "masculine," and *nonbinary* just means outside the dichotomy of masculine or feminine, either both or neither. "When I first got into the witch community, the hetero witches were all pushing me to embrace my inner goddess because I was born biologically female." Major eye roll. "Fuck that."

Eowyn nods in sympathy. "Part of what we're trying to do is de-gender magic," she tells me. "There hasn't been a major update on a lot of magical thinking around gender since the early 1900s, and a lot of the goddess movement that's supposed to be pro-woman power ends up excluding folks who don't fit the binary." She's working on a new product line she calls "Godex Hirself!"

Saul was at the house for a full-moon ritual the weekend before, and they brought their partner. Saul says, "He's been a solitary witch since he was thirteen or something, so it was kind of a lot for him to be in a whole room of queer witches."

"They come from a generation where queer is something you are on the internet," Meff, Eowyn's partner, interjects. "I'm from a generation where queer is something you are in your body. It's how people react when you walk down the street." Meff thumps their chest. You get the sense that they've thrown fists to defend their gender expression before.

Eowyn and Saul talk about the multitude of witch shops in town, which are undergoing something of a renaissance: "There's this minimalist new age place, they got written up by *Vogue*. Oh, and there's a Norse magic place run by Nazis!" I'm stunned for a moment, but the witches explain that white supremacists seeking symbols to build a history and mythology for their blood-and-soil nationalism and old-school masculinity have co-opted Scandinavian mythology. German Nazis were into paganism too, and Norse runes have less of a knee-jerk reaction than swastikas as American fascists seek new recruits. "Ethnic European mythology" is the sell. Eowyn's "Ain't afraid of no ghosts or fascists" patch is a real statement, it turns out, and she is constantly monitoring her online pagan communities for the dog whistles of Nazism. Eowyn and Meff talk about Antifa not as a news story, but as a piece of daily life.

Suddenly, everything seems more serious. There is a three-way battle going on for the soul of magic, between Warner Bros.' corporate fandom and new age spiritualists and neo-Nazis. But Eowyn's community is yet another faction, finding its feet in a curated selection of pagan practices, a collection of trans and non-binary folk who are turning to magic as a space to be "the other." Everyone is trying to make meaning, to carve out their own identity through a shared ritual with history.

"Witchcraft really is about heresy," Eowyn tells me, "daring to go against the established social order. In Europe, heretics and witches were burned with little distinction. It was just assumed that people had an array of magical powers, some divine, some not." Throughout my visit Eowyn's sense of the historical impresses me. I may not believe in her magic, but I have to admit she's done her research. Eowyn, who grew up Quaker, went to college for religious studies, and talks gleefully about a class on the sacred and sacrifice. "Sacrifice happens when something doesn't belong in the system, or defies categorization," she says. "It becomes sacred, and then is eliminated to reinforce categories. You're either on the pedestal, or under the bus."

The next night, a WitchPunx member named Canis, who Eowyn refers to as her apprentice, comes over to give Meff a new tattoo. They trace the lines of a mugwort plant on Meff's collarbone. A member of the daisy family, mugwort is a prickly protective plant that was used as an insecticide in ancient gardens and worn by Roman soldiers in their sandals to protect against fatigue. Meff tells me that they smoke mugwort as an aide to creativity, because it acts as a mild hallucinogen to promote lucid dreaming and astral projection. Art and magic are all interlinked, and even the ink Canis is using to make the tattoo has been mixed with ash from a ritual. Mugwort, I later learn, is considered a noxious weed and is illegal to plant in many states.

Canis grew up in a speaking-in-tongues miracle church here in Massachusetts. They have tattoos of runes on their knuckles and two eyes (one open, one closed) on their knees, and wear dangly hoop earrings with what look like real bird claws hanging off of them. Their long, dyed hair is mashed down by an army cap, and their face is obscured by big glasses. They wear a graphic T-shirt of a vulture with a crown of roses.

"I'm looking at doing manual labor in a sewage treatment plant," they tell us as they trace Meff's tattoo and the witches' menagerie of seven cats come in and out of the room. "It's good pay but hard on the body." Canis is anxious about being able to afford to continue testosterone treatments. They dropped out of school a few years ago and have been working odd jobs. Tattoo is a world where they can carve out a niche as a trans person, helping people express themselves through images on their bodies. Their apprenticeship with Eowyn has been less spell casting, as I'd expect, and more a business crash course in making and selling jewelry—what Eowyn calls "radical adornment." In a world of fluid bodies and chosen gender expressions, I realize, what people choose to wear, from tattoos to clothing, is a way both of creating self and of finding community. It isn't casual, and in a world that isn't friendly to all expressions, it can literally be life or death.

Canis puts on a playlist to work to.

"What are we listening to?" Meff asks.

"It's a D&D soundtrack," Canis says. "Apocalypse World."


II.

Over the weekend, I head with Eowyn and Meff to New Jersey, where they are vendors as part of a festival in a city park. The day is hot and clear, and the witches open their suitcases on their sides in their booth, revealing a ready-to-go display of jewelry: crystal pendants and miniature meat cleaver earrings and one necklace that says "sodomite" between two evil eyes. An array of pins is scattered beneath them, with messages ranging from "ask my pronouns" to "spooky kid."

In front of the suitcases of jewelry are a range of soaps, creams, "legal smokeable" blends of mugwort and flowers, and, at the end of the table, a perfect plastic replica of a giant monitor lizard. It's about a foot long, gray-green, and disconcertingly life-like. "That's Carl," the witches tell the kids and credulous adults who come up not to buy anything but to see if the lizard is real. "He's our head of sales." It's their version of the typewriter, a gimmick to lure people in.

There are eight vendors at the park in New Jersey, all selling some level of jewelry (often featuring small animal bones), crystals, and witchy handcrafts, but Eowyn and Meff's table is consistently the busiest. On the stage in front of the vendors, a middle-aged woman leads Zumba, a hipster band plays an acoustic set, and a young white organizer raps about positivity.

A young, grinning man with curly hair and a single earring comes up, just on the edge of flamboyant but shy. Eowyn drops immediately into a conversation with him about horror movies and by the end she is custom making him another single earring with a crow skull dangling from the end. Like me at the typewriter, she susses out points of connection for each person who comes to the table. For little girls in summer dresses, she asks if they know their birthstones and shows them necklaces. A cardiologist approaches, and the two bargain over a pin featuring an anatomical heart. Eowyn shows two young women necklaces shaped like meat cleavers and tells them that they're to ward off street harassment.

"I want everyone to find themselves on my table," Eowyn tells me. To see their passions reflected, and gain the gift, through a bit of capitalist magic, of being able to name themselves, to physicalize their identity, and so to call what they want to be into being.

Eowyn says everyone who's vending is selling a story. "We're from Salem, Mass," Eowyn and Meff say to everyone who approaches them, first thing, taking a bit of the mystique of that place with them. Salem is one of the good stories. It's cheesy and New England when you're actually there but enticing enough from the outside through the draw of history, the mystique of superstition.

Outside of Salem, Eowyn says, "a big part of what we do is being visibly queer in public space." By signaling that they are "other," the witches are, in effect, creating a pop-up queer community wherever they go. In communities for whom it's not always safe to be forthcoming with their place of birth, romantic history, gender identity, or job, magic can be a way to assert identity that's within a queer person's control.

When other systems of categorization fail or are weaponized to hurt queer people, astrology and magical systems of categorization can be a way, in the words of the authors of an anonymous *n+1* article, of "giving the slip," a middle finger to mainstream taxonomies of identity. "For all the Americans who think astrology is 'not at all scientific,' there are other unpolled Americans who believe gender is not at all scientific," *n+1* asserts. "Queer followers of astrology make the comparison easy to draw: 'Is Alex a man or a woman?' Alex is an Aries."

The day of the New Jersey market, I start off by getting breakfast with literary world friends and take them to meet the witches afterward. Approaching the Holy Crow table, I feel like a translator. I'm a fellow skeptic to my literary friends, but to the witches, I'm a fellow traveler on the road of hustle, a fellow "reader," psychic or not.

Pushing down my insecurities that my poetry is providing the same service of useful unreality as fortune-telling, I perch awkwardly on a chair next to Carl the lizard with my typewriter. An older German woman with a dog comes up to me. Her topic, of course, is "positive energy." I direct her to the witches while I write, and she ends up buying a hundred dollars of charms from them before her poem is done.

"I tell the kids all the time that being a witch is a service job," Eowyn says. For the German mom who spends a hundred dollars on queer punk American magic jewelry in a park in New Jersey, I write:

You follow the ley lines
across continents, pick up
fellow travelers but forget
the luggage, sometimes.
    Who needs it? No bag
can carry what you seek,

no sleek suitcase but the
  messy complications of trees
    with deep roots and legends
in their bark,
  becoming fossils
or passing into song,
  but living, you understand,
  still living through every breath we take,
each moment deliberate.
No sacred land, only what
  we make of it.
We speak, and the water
        answers.

I realize it's less about believing or not in magic than it is about what stories we find interesting—which ones we choose to tell, and, in so telling, remind ourselves of who we are.

A few months before my trip to visit the witches, I drove to Missouri to visit my grandparents in the house where I'd hatched RENT Poet many years ago. As usual, the visit centered around their dining room table, where my grandmother sipped cranberry juice from a straw with shaking hands. She wasn't much of a conversationalist anymore—she always had a big smile for me but often had to be prompted to speak, and you could tell that took a huge mental effort.

A momentary silence fell while my grandfather bustled with food in the kitchen, and in that silence, my eye fell on something that I'd never seen in that house before. On top of a pile of stuff on a chair was a faded, hand-painted sign:

MADAME

SYLVIA

"well versed and good hearted"

FIND OUT YOUR

DESTINY FROM

WORLD FAMOUS PALM READER!

(for a small donation)

Under the words I saw a photograph, faded from time, of a woman in a floppy hat and red shawl. She sat on a lawn chair opposite a second person, staring intently at their palm.

"Hey, Grandma Robin," I asked. "Who is Madame Sylvia?"

"Me," she replied.

No one had ever mentioned this side of my grandma—the palm reader. My parents are hardcore rationalists, and the story I'd learned split her life in two chapters: first, the brilliant trailblazing professor in an age when women were just breaking into academia, who gave her name only as "Doctor Remington" at all-male academic clubs and then dared them not to seat her when she showed up with visiting dignitaries. Women did not do political science. She did political science. Women did not run academic departments. Fine. She'd just be the first, then.

But the Robin I knew was softer. She'd drawn back from public life and now held drum circles in her house and kept a Goddess of the Day calendar. I'd been led to believe that a series of breakdowns before I was born led her to retire and find solace in seeking some form of spiritual practice. But the faded photograph of my grandmother in her PhD prime, set up on the street as a palm reader, told a different story. That both of these selves were inside her the whole time.

After dinner, my grandma's niece got out a pack of cards. Growing up far from my grandparents, I'd never known this cousin well. She was a blond wisp a few decades my senior, with a quick tongue and easy laugh. The cards she got out were not regular playing cards. These had a picture on top of an eagle in a dreamcatcher, and the words "Medicine Cards" in big letters on the side. "Would you read our fortunes," my cousin asked, "Madame Sylvia?"

Something changed about my grandmother the moment she held the medicine cards. She could not stand or walk or even form more than a few words on her own without assistance, but her shaking hands seemed to steady as she slid the deck from the box, like her body remembering a practiced move. She offered the deck to each of us, and we pulled our animals one at a time for a reading: jaguar, horse, fox, owl, weasel. No matter what card we pulled, as each person revealed what was in their hand, she'd say, "Ah, that's a very powerful animal!"

With the cards on the table next to her, Grandma Robin gained a new authority, as if her eyes had become sharper. Here, in the after-dinner glow, she owned the room. She read in a croaky voice from a book that interpreted each card with stories about the animals they showed, alongside warnings and advice on love—I imagine, at one time, she'd have put her own spin on these stories, half memorizing them to paint whole worlds with her words. Now, she just read.

Sometimes, Robin's eyes slipped out of focus and away to that world only folks in their twilight years can see. She was getting tired. Her niece would take over reading for a moment, but before long the retired professor would summon her strength and resume. Their voices would join together for a moment, across generations. By the end of the night, Robin's voice was hoarse, and she'd sip cranberry juice between readings, still passing the cards to the next person at the table for them to draw an animal until the night got late and we all fell into bed. She could have kept going, easily.

It was the most I'd heard my grandmother speak in years.

The cards let my grandmother read, not for herself (she'd lost interest in that long ago) but for another person, as a gift to each of us sitting around that table. It was a chance to let us know that she *saw* us, even if she couldn't express much. The cards let her tap into a bigger conversation, the conversation of what sort of people we were.

I was a horse, I believe. My dad was . . . a fox? Maybe? Hard to remember, it's not my mythology.

But the next morning, though her voice was shot, my grand-mother sat at the dining room table after breakfast with the medi-cine card book open in front of her, reading intently, with the owl card clutched in her hand: the card of magic and wisdom. It was the card she had chosen for herself, the night before.

## III.

My grandmother is in my mind throughout my visit with the witches in Salem. Each day, like my grandmother, Eowyn has to lie down for a while in the afternoon. She has a chronic condition that leaves her in crippling pain much of the time. While Eowyn's public gender expression is more straightforwardly femme, her disability puts her body firmly into the "other" category within the gender binary.

In the evenings, after dinner, Eowyn and Meff sit in the living room with paper calendars and go through the markets they are planning to vend at in coming weeks and months—the work part of magic never ends. Lounging around after finishing, Eowyn calls Meff "grandpa" in response to some grouchy comment, and we all laugh. "I see you in a wide-brimmed hat with a cane, out on the porch . . ." I tell Meff.

"Yeah," they reply, "that's one of my genders."

I understand, in that moment, a nuance of the plural pronoun "they." Our media is saturated with stories of trans people transitioning *between* genders, male and female. But "they" is perfect because it can mean more than just male or female. It's not that Meff subscribes to team man or team woman, or even to neither team, it's that their gender expression is expansive.

I'd read my Judith Butler in college and was comfortable with the idea of gender as a performance, a way of acting in relationship to other people. But I hadn't taken this to its logical theater-kid extreme: If gender is a performance, then each character's unique performance of it can be classed as its own gender; "grandpa" can be a gender. Eowyn winks and revels in the fact that she is "daddy" in many of her relationships—a role where she doesn't take on a masculine pronoun, but a way of speaking that acknowledges a character she enjoys taking on in the bedroom. And I can see the "daddy" energy in daily life too, in the way she makes decisions for herself and Meff, the way she lovingly gives orders.

"You have an astral mustache, sometimes," Eowyn tells Meff.

The younger trans folk I meet in the WitchPunx Collective are preoccupied with their physical bodies, taking testosterone and binding breasts. The idea of an astral mustache is something else, an affirmation that some things don't need to be physicalized to be real.

I spoke with Eowyn the year before while she was touring through California about having "astral sex" while on the road vending, physically distant from her partners. I kept trying to figure out what this was in terms I understood—were they sexting? But Eowyn insisted that, no, they were connected psychically and able to manipulate each other's astral bodies in erotic ways and feel it without even talking.

We all grin at the idea of an astral mustache, but whether or not I believe in astral anything, I know the function of this concept is real for this couple. For Eowyn and Meff, a couple who are respectively disabled and trans, what's real goes constantly beyond the realm of the physical. I wonder if this framework is in part a generational difference between them and the young trans WitchPunx, who grew up as part of a generation with assessable and relatively well-understood surgical modification and so perhaps have less need for astral bodies. In Salem, Eowyn tells me that astral sex isn't just for when she's traveling and far from her partner's body, but also a part of her ordinary sex. In line, I guess, with being "daddy" in bed, she tells me that she loves fucking her partners with her "astral cock."

"But what are you doing *physically* while doing the astral stuff?" I ask.

"Oh, you know," she says with a laugh, "fucking."

Part of me instinctively understands. I've dated both genders and fallen legitimately in love with brains and kindness but have often fantasized about bodies different from the one in front of me. I remember having shame about fantasizing during sex with both genders, too embarrassed to bring it up with a partner. The fantasy didn't replace or even get in the way of the physical sensations, it just built on them with an imagined world that only I could see. "Of course," Eowyn tells me when I share this thought, "everything is in our brains." Our brains are physical, so even a fantasy can change reality. Why should we dismiss something as lesser because other things have more extrinsic stimulus?

"I do a lot of sex magic, but I don't tell the kids about that as much," Eowyn says. Her WitchPunx Collective are mostly in their late teens and early twenties. "People will ask how I cast spells, and I'll say I just do!"

In a discourse of magic so closely linked to queerness, it makes sense that sex is a pivotal element. I think back to witch panics and the ideas of witches as sexually deviant women and remember Eowyn laughing at the Witch Museum's insistence that magic isn't real, and that witchcraft should be considered a religion like any other.

"I don't understand any religion that doesn't have an *ecstatic* component," she'd said to me. "Men in robes? No thanks." The word *ecstatic* comes from an ancient Greek word meaning something like "to be carried away." I have a vision of bacchanalias, sacred ritual dances that ended in orgies, and of the little I knew about spirit possession in African diasporic traditions, where individuals could lose themselves in the characters of spirits, spurred on by drums and dancing. The ancient Greek origin of the word *ecstasy* could be translated as "to displace," though a literal translation would be closer to "to stand out."

My time with the witches struck me as so different from how I'd interacted with the queer community before, which if I'm being honest was mostly online. I came of age on the internet, and quickly found gay forums. I never posted in my early years, still young enough to know that strangers—especially strangers online—were potentially dangerous and shouldn't be engaged. I was a lurker, but I would read every back and forth on the early 2000s message boards raptly, forming a model for desire and community from behind the protection of a screen. But to access that community, I never had to talk, never had to engage and put myself out there.

I was afraid of being gay. I came from a liberal family in a liberal state and even my godparents were gay, but there it was. I built my armor well—I passed in most contexts. Growing up so different already, as an only child without a TV and then as an expat, the last thing I ever wanted to do was set any more markers of difference between myself and as many other people as I could cleave onto. What I didn't realize was that those markers of difference are how subcultures find each other and form.

Maybe it's like this for all queer people who haven't discovered that they have a history yet. Maybe for all people whose history isn't taught in schools. If there is no future for people like you, you mold yourself into people who have a future, whose pasts are known and assured, if you can. I could. I learned the term for this in my twenties: *passing privilege*. I could be queer when it suited me, pass when it did not. Mostly it did not.

Even as an adult, I'd rarely sought out queer company explicitly, getting some overlap with the artists and travelers I counted as my close friends, but not making these conversations central to my relationships. I hadn't thought about what it would mean for me to spend this physical time with the queer community. During my time with the witches, I painted my nails with them, marking myself out physically as queer for the first time, bringing it into my body. "Radical adornment." When I got home, I started seeking out queer open mics and started my own explicitly queer group of typewriter poets. There was a piece of myself I saw in the witches, a story I had been estranged from without knowing it.

Sitting with Eowyn, I wrote a poem half for her, and half for me, following a discussion of the way queerness inevitably shows up in monsters, in the outcasts of our stories:

This is a manifesto for vampires
unseen in mirrors,
encountering themselves
in camp 70s horror with a glow
    of recognition,
always rooting for the monsters
  who are at least honest
    to themselves, at least
not pretending altruism.
Fallen but still loud.
And the heroes all blend
into one another but we remember
        our stories by their
            villains.

This is the truth High School
goths know, maybe, booming
through the silence, pain
and ecstasy the same on
the face and who are we to
say what another is experien
                         cing
      as they
shapeshift?

## IV.

Thunderclouds appear in the sky and lightning cracks as we drive
out of Salem on my final day with the witches. Eowyn has a few
final things she wants to show me before I go. "They may close
the pond before we get there," Eowyn tells me, "but I still want
you to see it." A lake, larger than I imagined, appears behind the
trees ahead of us. I catch my breath—not because of the place
itself, but because of what it means.

We round the trees and are at Walden Pond.

Words I didn't know were still buried in my brain from high
school spring into my mind, like the place itself is animating
them: "I came to the woods because I wanted to live deliberately,
to live deep and suck the marrow out of life." I'd never talked
to Eowyn about Thoreau, but he was my first brush with phi-
losophy and ecology as a teenager. Encountering the transcen-

dentalists in eleventh grade American literature lit a fire under my ass that would have me Wikipedia searching philosophical movements instead of paying attention in Spanish class, and listening to iTunes U lectures on the nature of reality for the rest of high school when I should have been doing my homework. How could it be that there was an entire field of study devoted to knowing what is real, and what is good, and that I'd never even heard of it?

I walk alone right to the edge of the lake. Gaggles of tourists in bathing suits pass me coming down, escaping the looming rain, so now the shore is almost deserted. Eowyn stays in the car because the hill is steep, and it's been a hard month physically for her. Lifeguard stands loom emptily over the small beach, watching a line of buoys that encircle empty water, proof that people swim here in fairer weather. I imagine splashing families, piercing the woods with their loud desire to be a part of something ancient and famous, even while they tan.

But now it's quiet. As I stand at the water's edge, the sky above me breaks and thick drops pour down. I trace the forest skyline with my gaze, marveling at its jaggedness, marveling that I could stand here in the same woods, looking at the same sky, in the same New England rain, hundreds of years later. I stretch out my arms like a condor, and for a moment nothing else in the world exists.

I can see time, feel it dampening my skin. I don't know how long I stand there for.

- - -

There's something religious about being rained on in the quiet forest where Thoreau walked. "I thought you'd like that," Eowyn says with a grin when I get back to the car. She's built my last day with the witches into a pilgrimage especially for me, a final ritual to realize my own fandom, my own spiritual connection to a history, before I leave. Did she do it intentionally? Of course she did. She's not stupid. She's a witch.

We try to coordinate coming to Walden with Kevin the van poet, who's from Massachusetts and is currently wending his way through the state, but he's more interested in thrift shopping or getting pizza. Thoreau's stomping grounds were the site, I'm sure, of dozens of school field trips, a place perhaps of nostalgia but not of intrigue. A site of pilgrimage close to home is just another tourist trap. I recall my own disdain as an LA kid for the Hollywood Walk of Fame, the stars laden with dream symbolism that I now barely glance at, stumbling out of a comedy show or a bar. I've internalized what I need to know about impossible dreams already, maybe.

Eowyn intuited my magic, my history, my fandom. She makes me a pendant before I leave, two evil eyes around an anatomical human heart. "To see into others' hearts clearly while I'm writing," is my thought, but a visiting witch recognizes the evil eyes as protection and reads the piece as a warding off of my heart.

"It's both," Eowyn says, in her way. "It's important to keep your own heart safe, while working with the hearts of others."

Worn out from months of travel, still living job-to-job, uncertain in my future while telling people to go boldly into theirs, it's
exactly what I need to hear.

Even as I haul a twenty-pound portable typewriter built eighty
years ago around the country with me, I've always struggled to
see myself in the "America" of the history books. Historical reen-
actors with their muskets are thick on the ground in Lexington
and Concord, a stone's throw from Salem, the places where the
first shots of the American Revolution were fired. "History itself
is a ritual," Eowyn says, "it's a question of which rituals we affirm
and which we leave."

The language of history as a ritual stirs me, one more marker
on the path I'm trying to tread as a poet between the stories and
magic. Both seem to me to be an interpretive layer over our reality
that doesn't just observe that reality but also bends and shapes
it. Magic and poetry are both the refusal of explanation, an exploration of the edges of comprehensibility bounded by tradition
and ritual, acting not in their historical context but in people's
immediate lives.

After Walden Pond, Eowyn takes me to Authors' Ridge. This
is where Thoreau and Emerson and Hawthorne and Alcott are
buried. Eowyn knows me, at this point, knows I'm happy to en-
tertain mugwort and occult knowledge but that they aren't going to stir my blood. But here, I can't help but be moved by the
offerings visitors have left in front of the tombstones: pens and

pencils and a bird's nest for Thoreau, a piled mini-cairn of stones for Emerson, a deluge of pens for Alcott. It's a part of history I can cleave to and claim.

This was what she wanted to show me—what people leave at writers' graves.

# Document/ed

## with poems by Jeremias Leonel Estrada Aguilar and translation by Ana Reynoso

| | |
|---|---|
| *Escucha nada más* | *Just listen,* |
| *Unos momentos.* | *For a moment.* |
| *Será la última petición,* | *This will be my last request,* |
| *Para que escuches a mi corazón.* | *For you to listen to my heart.* |

Before I started writing poems on the street, I had little interest in poetry. I was an actor—but when I began to write as a public performance, I knew I'd have to start researching my "character." An actor prepares! So I attended readings, picked up books of poetry, audited classes, made poetry friends. These friends introduced me sometimes in casual conversation as "Rent Poet," as if in recognition that the Brian in front of them wasn't a poet, he just played one. The typewriter was my tool to lure people who weren't interested in poetry into engaging with it, but it had an unexpected consequence.

Poets started finding me.

As an only child with no family nearby, Thanksgiving dinners at my parents' house have always been a hodgepodge affair of chosen family and friends, close or distant, without somewhere else to be for the holiday. In 2018, I met one of my father's former students, Maria Elena, as we waited for the turkey to come out of the oven. Maria Elena said, "I've actually been wanting to talk to you—I've been working with a Guatemalan asylum seeker, Jeremias, who wrote a book of poems while in immigration detention. Would you be interested in reading what he's written and helping us think about what comes next? Poetry isn't my expertise."

For years I had been masquerading as a poet, and funny what happens when you tell a story about yourself often enough: people start to believe it. Suddenly I wasn't just an anonymous typewriter, but a representative of the whole world of poetry for people knocking on that door. I was so used to thinking of myself as a literary outsider that it was strange to be on the other side, a gatekeeper with a newfound responsibility to hold open the door I'd found.

A mentor had been talking to me about "literary citizenship" as the obligation that writers have to support each other's work and work to elevate each other's voices. He'd ask, "What does it mean to be a good literary citizen?" Extending that logic, what did it mean to be a good citizen, period, in an age of immigration terror and child detention? Looking at some poems seemed like the very smallest place to start.

Following that Thanksgiving dinner, Maria Elena brought me with her to visit the Theo Lacy Facility, the detention center (also, fun fact, maximum-security prison) where detainee poet Jeremias spent most of the months of his asylum plea. Theo Lacy blends in disturbingly well in suburban Orange County, California, a cute clock-tower facade disguising the entrance to the massive maximum-security prison. It's opposite a TGI Friday's and a mega-mall. Five miles down the road is Disneyland, "The Happiest Place on Earth."

Jeremias had lost his appeal and been deported only a few months before I learned his story, and was in Mexico when Maria Elena and I visited Theo Lacy. It was Maria Elena's first time back to the facility since Jeremias had gone, and that meant she'd be meeting a new asylum seeker. Maria Elena was a member of Friends of Orange County Detainees, who visit people waiting for their immigration cases to be heard. Detainees put their name on a list if they want to receive a visit from a stranger—they know that person isn't a lawyer, just a willing ear. And for many detainees, scared and isolated and cut off from the outside world, that's enough.

Maria Elena had visited Jeremias for over a year, and now, just like that, he was gone. She fought nerves in the lobby as we waited, readying herself to meet a new stranger, to encounter a new story that she would promise to show up for, to invest herself in, no matter what. I found myself humbled, thinking about the few minutes of space I'd hold for people at my typewriter. In visiting inmates, writing letters back and forth until strangers became friends, Maria Elena was holding that space for years.

Maria Elena's grandparents are from Nicaragua and she does immigration research in public health, which she says is all population based, working with data on a massive scale about millions of anonymous lives. As our wait to get beyond the waiting room at Theo Lacy stretched into hours, Maria Elena told me, "I heard a speaker say something at a conference that really impacted me: you have to learn to love the $n$." In data science, the $n$ is the variable for the number of people impacted—but it's just a number, it has no human face. "One of my data sets has 1.8 million people," Maria Elena said. "I wanted direct, individualized contact with the people whose lives I'd be impacting. It was a way for me not to lose my soul while doing my PhD."

Since 2014, for as long as I'd been writing poetry for thousands of strangers, Maria Elena had been steadfastly visiting one person at a time at Theo Lacy through the end of their case, which usually meant their deportation. She likened it to a friend who volunteered visiting elderly people on the verge of death in hospice—one moment they'd be there, the next they'd be gone.

"There's a loss of social citizenship that's almost like death," she said. Someone's entire network—job, family, neighborhood— could be vaporized in an instant, and with that a huge part of who they are. "It's people's self-image," she said. "I had someone I visited call me from Tijuana after he got deported. He'd lived in the US for over a decade, had his family here, and considered himself American more than anything. He called me, defeated, from the Mexican side of the border and said, 'Ya soy *Mexican*.'

Now I'm Mexican. Not Mejicano—Mexican. In English. Like he was on the outside, looking in." There was no pride in it. A piece of his identity had been stripped from him.

We sat for two and a half hours waiting to be called, watching families manage small children. After getting the name of the desired inmate, the guard at the counter asked, "Who is this person to you?"

"A friend," Maria Elena responded, though she'd never met this new man before in her life.

Many friends had passed through Theo Lacy. Before Jeremias, Maria Elena had visited an eighteen-year-old fleeing violence in Honduras, who had come to the US with Jeremias as part of the same caravan of immigrants seeking asylum. She knew Jeremias at first only by reputation: he was like the dad of the group, a little older and wiser, a backbone of emotional support for the young men, most just out of boyhood, who had traveled alongside him.

Jeremias tells me what it was like by phone, from Mexico. One by one, his caravan-mates were granted asylum or deported as they waited in Theo Lacy. When only he was left, he called Maria Elena. "I'm so happy for my friends," he told her, "but so sad to be all alone." The group had been a support system for the past six months in the facility, but Jeremias had been denied bond, so he had at least six more months to go. Inside the facility, with the threat that people could be taken away at any moment, it was hard to build any secure emotional support. So Jeremias turned to the outside world.

"The only one who visited me in those days was La Llorona," Jeremias recalls, chuckling at his own half joke. La Llorona is the Mexican boogeyman from folklore who wanders the land in a white dress, crying and looking for her lost children. When Maria Elena visited for the first time, Jeremias tells me, "We were strangers and it was awkward. She'd just ask, 'How did you eat?'" It took a while for them to strike up a rapport and learn to trust each other.

In my visit to Theo Lacy with Maria Elena, after Jeremias was gone, I witnessed this first meeting of strangers occur with the new detainee she'd promised to visit. The young man was relieved to have visitors, though he choked back tears half the time as we spoke through the glass. I have not included his name for privacy reasons, but am happy to report he has since been granted asylum.

He was still in his first month in the US seeking asylum, following his brother's murder and his own brutal beating at the hands of a gang back in Mexico. He was stricken with fear and had to pause to choke back tears every few minutes, but his words were a torrent bursting to get out, to make his story heard even if the person he was telling didn't have the power to do more than listen.

At the end of the visiting hour, a voice came on the PA system, and the phones shut off automatically. All we could see was the young man on the other side of the glass. Behind him, pencil markings tagged the walls in intricate calligraphy that I couldn't make out, inmates making their mark through writing in the only place where the inside and outside worlds met. Only one scratched phrase was clearly legible: "Fuck OC sheriff."

When we emerged, Maria Elena was shaking. "Did you see his wrist band?" she asked. "He'll never get out of solitary." She said that this band meant that her new friend had reported something to the guards in his first week at Theo Lacy, becoming a snitch in the eyes of other inmates. The guards put him in solitary "for his own protection," and there was no saying if he could ever be put back in with the other inmates. Maria Elena didn't say what we both knew: that long-term solitary confinement has been defined by the World Health Organization as a form of torture, as damaging to the psyche as physical brutality.

Visits are capped at thirty minutes for the general population, one hour for those in solitary. Letter writing, archaic in my every day, becomes a lifeline for those inside. "Era correspondencia de tortuga," Jeremias says. Turtle-speed mail.

Maria Elena was concerned about Jeremias's safety, because the Theo Lacy Facility was at the center of a federal investigation in 2017, resulting from a massive civil rights complaint over treatment of inmates. The charges ranged from withholding medicine to physical abuse. Maria Elena would ask about conditions inside, and in response Jeremias would send his poems, enclosed in letters, which he says are "about the madness of being locked up.

"Paper is difficult to find in prison, so I'd write in the margins of letters," Jeremias says when we speak on the phone. In the course of his fifteen months in a maximum-security prison waiting for his case to be heard, Jeremias wrote dozens of poems. "When others would throw their court letters away, I'd get them from the trash to use. I've always written," he says, "but no one was ever interested in the poems before, so I'd just end up throwing them away." Fighting his case now from the other side of the border, Jeremias still finds time to write poetry.

"In jail, you are just the number at the foot of your bed, not a human being. People know you by your number, not your name." He grows serious for a moment, searching for the words. "Writing poems was a way for me to reclaim my humanity."

*Anoche platiqué con el lucero*
*Que me alumbra mis noches por*
   *la ventana*
*Cuando las nubes se lo permiten.*

*Last night I talked to the bright star*
*That illuminates my nights*
   *through the window*
*When the clouds give him a chance.*

*Y me preguntó,*
*¿por qué esa mirada triste?*
*Y yo, entre lágrimas y sollozos, le dije,*
*Que el encierro me abate hasta el*
   *alma.*
*Quisiera estar tan libre como él,*
*Para observar a todo el mundo.*
*Quisiera darle calor a mis seres*
   *amados,*

*He asked,*
*Why the sad look?*
*Between sobs, I told him*
*That imprisonment shuts down*
   *my soul*
*That I would like to be free, like him*
*To watch the whole world*
*And give warmth to my loved*
   *ones,*

| | |
|---|---|
| *así como él lo hace con sus rayos.* | *The way he does with his rays,* |
| *Quisiera guiar a todos los que* | *And guide the ones I love,* |
| *yo amo,* | *The way he guides all of the* |
| *así como él guía a todos los viajeros.* | *wanderers.* |

In his letters to Maria Elena, Jeremias would always say, "I think I'm going crazy," before sharing his poems. At first I thought this was a classic poet move, excusing his work as crazy to shield when he shared a deep part of himself. I soon learned it went deeper than that. Jeremias didn't call his writing poems, he called them "mis inspiraciones," which can mean inspirations, but also means breaths, as if the writing was an act of inhaling.

Immigration detainees don't have the rights to access the classes and activities that even maximum-security prisoners with citizenship have, so the detainees have to find their own ways to not go mad with boredom. "The majority of people in prison pass the time with exercise, basketball or volleyball, or reading," Jeremias tells me. "One friend I made in there sang, and we would have a concert every night. When he started singing, everyone would join in. Together, we invented La Chochona Radio Station!"—I had to look up the word *chochona*. It means "crybaby."

"We'd have announcements and music," Jeremias says. Of course, the inmates didn't have access to recording equipment or transmission—their radio station was made up of their bodies and voices, creating entertainment for each other into the night. "There was a Salvadoran in detention with us who had money, and he'd buy chocolate and Doritos from the commissary so we could have prize giveaways. We'd have impersonation singing competitions, with songs from Juan Gabriel, Vicente Fernández, and Enrique Iglesias. We'd award four places—gold, silver, bronze, and *palo* (wooden stick). But everyone got the same chocolate in the end!

"I shared my poems on the radio too. I remember sharing one, 'Libertad,' about the pain of separation. Everyone in there had felt that pain, and everyone went to bed crying that night. We said it was the saddest night of Crybaby Radio."

*Estando con mis compas—*
*El 34—el 47—el 21 y el 5—*
*Componiendo unas rolas*
*Para pasar la noche*
*Y olvidar nuestras penas.*

*Hanging with my buddies—*
*34—47—21 and 5—*
*Composing some songs*
*To get through the night*
*And forget my sorrows.*

*El compa 96 sólo decía*
*Ya no vengo a este lado*
*Porque me voy a volver*
*Loco muy loco.*

*My buddy 96 would say*
*I won't come to this side*
*Because I'm going to turn*
*Crazy so crazy.*

*El 47 es pintor del futuro*
*Porque pinta cosas raras*
*Y este noche estamos*
*Locos muy locos*
*Porque mañana no se sabe,*
*Paisano loco, paisano loco.*

*47 is a painter of the future*
*Because he paints strange things*
*And tonight we are*
*Crazy so crazy*
*Because tomorrow is uncertain*
*My crazy brother, my crazy brother.*

| | |
|---|---|
| *Y la comida de gato* | *And cat food* |
| *Y la boloña podrida* | *And spoiled bologna* |
| *Te vuelve* | *Will drive you* |
| *Loco muy loco.* | *Mad so mad.* |

"Sometimes they'd serve us cat food in prison," Jeremias says, explaining the final stanza of this poem. "No disrespect to the little cats," he adds.

Reading Jeremias's poems, I was forced to confront a darker side of art. On first hearing his story, it struck me that the poems and competitions were a form of resilience, people with nothing creating for each other, finding community in dire straits as a way to preserve their humanity. But Jeremias's poems speak in a different way—the singing and dancing around, the writing of grand verses, not just as a connection with the core of human dignity but as an expression of madness itself, as if art is humanity leaving the body, not just a breath in but a breath out.

Was Jeremias's work an expression of inner nobility and deep thought in legacy with the great imprisoned writers of history, or the ranting and dancing of the homeless man by the roadside who has been cast out by society and speaks to himself all day long? Of all the poems in the book, this one troubles me the most, because it seems to pull back the curtain and show that writing can be both. It breaks down the division I want to place between madness and sanity, between coping and creativity. Jeremias wasn't just saying he was crazy. He knew he had been driven mad by imprisonment, and this outpouring of art was the result. I was so invested in the idea of art as healing, I had missed that art can also be a symptom, a madness for documenting the world with words, that we call "being a writer."

It made me wonder, what if imprisoned writers Cervantes or Thoreau hadn't been taken seriously, hadn't had the right friends in literary circles? Like Jeremias's early poems, perhaps the scraps of paper they had written on would have been discarded.

Maria Elena's keenness on Jeremias's poems makes sense to me when I learn that her undergraduate degree is in testimonial Spanish literature. "Jeremias's poems were deeply painful to receive," she says, "because I got them in real time. He'd tell me what he was experiencing, and then I'd get these inner thoughts." But Maria Elena didn't just passively read the poems. Aside from being a springboard for discussion about Jeremias's situation, she would give feedback on his writing, challenging him to stretch himself in his descriptions and metaphors. "Princess again?" she'd tease him. "I'm sure you can come up with a better word!" It became a game they played, a shared project to make the long boring hours more bearable.

After receiving and workshopping dozens of poems, Maria Elena and a friend typed them all up, and Maria Elena sent Jeremias the combined works with a formal "revise and resubmit" letter based on what she'd seen in the academic publishing world.

And Jeremias's response? "He called me cracking up!" Maria

Elena says. "He thought it was hilarious." Jeremias laughs talking about it even now. This day labor construction worker from Guatemala was being asked by someone at a major university to write a book—the thought of it!

The book, small and bound with blue construction paper, was the reward Maria Elena offered on a GoFundMe page she made to raise money for Jeremias's deportation proceedings. His poetry, in the right hands, helped Jeremias raise two thousand dollars for legal fees. Were people giving to the art or to the cause? In this case, perhaps there wasn't a difference.

"For literature to exist, there is always a power dynamic," Maria Elena tells me. "Between someone who has a story to tell and someone who has the power to put it in front of a broader audience."

But Maria Elena shoos away any notion of a savior complex. "The question for me is, what does it look like to create a friendship within the dynamic of such an unequal power relationship?" she says. She tells me the best she's been able to do is try to listen without judgment, be honest about who she is, why she's visiting people, and how she plans to stay in touch. "And, most importantly, following up on promises," she says. "It's about setting and managing expectations."

I think of my own tendency to want to please, to take on too much at once. The typewriter let me manage my involvement in people's stories, to confine them to a four-inch by six-inch piece of paper and a single draft. But the deeper I got into people's stories, the harder it became to put them down—and the more I found I didn't want to.

The book Maria Elena helped Jeremias assemble and distribute tells the story of his time in prison and his longing for his wife in simple but powerful language. As a young man over a decade ago, Jeremias had crossed the border for the first time, looking for work. He met his wife, Lorena, in the US, at the Evangelical church they both attended in Riverside, California. "When I first asked my wife out, she said no," Jeremias confides to me, laughing. "She said my face looked like a newborn baby, I was so young!"

Jeremias had little formal education or English, and so worked in construction, while Lorena worked as a housekeeper. He says that when she finally agreed to go on a date with him, he didn't have the money to take her to a nice restaurant, so they began their relationship in a Chinese buffet. It was simple, but it worked. Half of the poems Jeremias wrote from detention were love poems for Lorena:

| | |
|---|---|
| *Recuerdo como si fue ayer* | *I remember it as if it were yesterday* |
| *El día que te robé* | *The first day I stole* |
| *Por primera vez un beso.* | *A kiss from you.* |
| *Recuerdo tu sonrisa inocente* | *I remember your innocent smile* |
| *En tu bello rostro.* | *On your beautiful face.* |

| | |
|---|---|
| *Recuerdo que no dijimos nada.* | *I remember we said nothing.* |
| *Solamente se cruzaron nuestras miradas* | *Only our gazes crossed* |
| *Y yo sabía* | *And I knew I had found happiness.* |
| *Que había* | |
| *Encontrado la felicidad.* | |

The couple had two kids, Jeremy and Jessie, both born American citizens. I asked Jeremias how he had come to be detained and he told me that he had actually never intended to return to the US after he and his family left in 2015.

Deportations under the Obama administration were already at an all-time high, and it was a calculated decision by the family to return rather than live in anxiety at the threat of deportation— the children were still young, and on top of that, Jeremias's father in Guatemala had fallen ill and needed caring for. Jeremias says he imagined raising his children to play soccer on the same streets where he grew up.

But when the family got to Nueva Concepción in Guatemala, they found the city rocked by violence from police in cahoots with the drug lords. Never one to sit idly by, Jeremias got involved in activism against state corruption, and the state clamped down. Jeremias's group staged peaceful protests that led to the investigation and imprisonment of the corrupt chief of police, and in retribution the mayor sent armed men to threaten Jeremias's and other protestors' families. "That was the blow that broke the vase," Jeremias tells me, recalling with horror how neighbors had stopped men from kidnapping his son. "We got on the bus to go north." Whatever uncertainty was before them had to be better than the clear threat they were leaving behind.

What was going on in Guatemala was not divorced from American policy and action. In the 1960s, while King and Chavez marched for civil rights domestically, the US, terrified of communism in the new world, intervened abroad across Latin America to crush popular revolutions in favor of capitalist leaders and dictators who would operate with US interests in mind. In Guatemala, the civil war lasted from 1960 to 1996, destabilizing the country and allowing corruption like the kind Jeremias faced at the local level to take hold. In Nicaragua, where Maria Elena's grandparents were from, the US backed Contra terrorists throughout the 1980s in an attempt to overthrow the socialist government.

Before US interventionism in the second half of the twentieth century, immigration across the southern border had mostly been Mexican itinerant workers who'd come across for work and go home to their families when the season ended. "The border crossed us," a common saying goes, reflecting the reality that much of the Southwest was once part of Mexico, and many families lived and worked historically on both sides of the border. Ironically, increased security at the border led to more people staying in the US without papers rather than fewer and more bringing families over because they knew if they left, they might not be able to come back. Central American migration, a more recent pattern, has focused less on work and more on asylum seekers looking for safety in the country that had destabilized their home countries.

Before making their way back to the US border, Jeremias's family tried to settle in his wife's native state of Chiapas, Mexico, in 2016. Here, when Jeremias went to register his son in school, he discovered that his wife and her Mexican citizenship had been purged from the system as part of a move toward voter suppression. It was like she never existed at all. The mayor of the town ended up going to jail for purging people from local records, but again Jeremias and his family became political liabilities, and again they found men at the door, threatening them with guns.

Buoyed by the promise that, regardless of the political climate in the US, at least it was a land of laws and maybe even justice, Jeremias and his family decided to apply for asylum to return legally. When Jeremias was young, he'd crossed the desert on foot to enter illegally, but now, older and wiser, with a family to think about, he said he wanted to do things right. He had two kids who were American citizens and a legitimate fear for their lives. Even the pro bono lawyers at the border encouraged him to apply.

"We didn't know anything about asylum or refugee status at the time we came to the border," Jeremias says. "Immediately, there was a problem: my kids were born in the US and are US citizens." As of the time of writing, the laws around family detention and child custody in the US continue to become more restrictive. When Jeremias presented himself at the border, the laws that protected immigrant children from spending too much time in detention or being separated from their families for too long didn't apply to US-born children with immigrant parents. He learned that if the whole family wanted to cross, his US-citizen kids would not be able to stay with the family but would be placed in foster care indefinitely, forcibly separated from their parents, until the asylum case was settled.

Rather than split up the family further, Jeremias waited alone in the US for his case to be evaluated by the courts, while his wife, Lorena, and their two American-born kids went into hiding with nuns in Mexico, where the men who'd threatened them wouldn't find them. They were only able to speak to Jeremias occasionally, each side fearing for the safety of the other.

The separation would last fifteen long and painful months. Jeremias's love poems are tinged with heartbreak.

| | |
|---|---|
| *Como el desierto* | *Like the desert* |
| *Que necesita la lluvia,* | *Needs the rain,* |
| *así necesito de tu amor.* | *I need your love.* |
| *Aun sin saber* | *Even with not knowing* |
| *cuándo llegará la lluvia,* | *When the rain will come,* |
| *La espera con tanta necesidad.* | *It waits with such need.* |

| | |
|---|---|
| *Así mi corazón te buscará.* | *This is how my heart will search for you.* |
| *Así mi corazón te esperará.* | *This is how my heart will wait for you.* |

During the year separated from his family, waiting in detention, Jeremias heard stories other detainees told of wives leaving
their imprisoned husbands. Who could blame them? With no
guarantee of a release date, no way of knowing which country
their husbands would be released to, and no way for the men to
help support their families while in prison, separation too often
led to separation. In addition to the heartbreak of Jeremias's
poems, many express his anxiety, a longing tinged with fear.

*. . . si tú te vas*
*Mi corazón no lo soportaría*
*Y de un momento a otro se*
*    detendría.*

*. . . if you leave*
*My heart would not endure,*
*From one moment to another it*
*    would stop.*

*Porque la vida de mi ser*
*eres tú, preciosa mujer . . .*

*Because you are my life, my*
*    precious woman . . .*

*. . . si sigo así,*
*Lejos de ti, moriré.*

*. . . if I continue this way*
*Far from you, I will die.*

In the end, the judge denied Jeremias's asylum claim and deported him. Jeremias rejoined his family and relocated to Hidalgo,
in the south of Mexico, where Lorena's mother lives. Jeremias said
that when he made it back to his family, "I just got the biggest hug
I've ever felt. I came back with shaggy long hair—my kids asked
if it was really me." He made the decision to return and fight for
his citizenship with his family by his side in Mexico rather than

appeal the process in the US and spend indefinitely longer in a maximum-security prison. In Mexico, at least, he would have access to the internet and be able to communicate.

"My four-year-old recently asked me, 'Why is *my* country so bad?'" Jeremias tells me. His son knows he was born in the US and identifies as American, and there's something in the question that makes it sound like the little boy blames himself. Even at a young age, he is painfully, physically aware of the difference between himself and his parents—he is an American by law, and they are not. Jeremias's children are emblematic of a next generation of first-generation Americans, citizens of a country that's grown increasingly hostile to their parents and has broken their families apart.

Every day, Jeremias watches from the Mexican side of the border as Guatemalan families cross, hopeful for a better life in the north. "Work here is irregular, but good," Jeremias tells me. "We sell lunches to the ranches—bread, things like that." Never one to look back rather than forge ahead, Jeremias does not talk about the despair of realizing he'd spent a year in a brutal process that had yielded nothing. Only in his poems does he reveal this pain.

| | |
|---|---|
| *El día que me negaron la fianza* | *The day they denied me bail,* |
| *me morí . . .* | *I died . . .* |
| *Cuando venía a regreso,* | *As I came back,* |
| *venía muerto.* | *I came dead.* |
| *Hablaba sin pensar.* | *I spoke without thinking.* |
| *Tocaba sin sentir.* | *I touched without feeling.* |
| *La ilusión se murió.* | *The dream was dead.* |

"I still write poems and share them with Maria Elena," Jeremias tells me from the Mexican side of the border. "I can share them with you too, if you'd like! My wife always says, 'Pick up your papers, the kids are going to get into them!'"

Jeremias laughs.

"I'm not going to lie, I'm a little disorganized sometimes. But I am continuing my fight to return, sending emails to lawyers and organizations. Everyone is so busy, but I keep looking." Every day, Jeremias sends emails out, trying to find a lawyer who will represent his case pro bono. He is still searching. "They say the person who doesn't knock on the door never enters," he says, an old maxim teetering between optimism and despair. Jeremias knows that, whatever merits his story may have, the only way an attorney will pick his case up pro bono is if it has the potential to change policy more broadly. Even here, Jeremias is a number, and try to escape it though he might, his personal fight is political. He has no choice but to embrace that. "I want to open the door for many people," he says. "People who don't have all of my blessings."

Maria Elena had worked with an undergraduate student, Ana, to translate Jeremias's poems from Spanish to English. Ana told me that she saw the next step for the poems as working with an English-language poet to make the translations more poetic, so the rhythms and rhymes of the Spanish poetry sing. She asked me if I'd be willing to try my hand at it. I was uncertain, suggesting a few poets I know who come from Latino immigrant backgrounds, who might have a closer connection to the story, a better ear for the voice. Surely there would be other poets more qualified to work on Jeremias's poems.

"This is why we reached out to you, though," Ana told me.

"Who is the appropriate person to tell what story?" I wondered out loud, wanting to be respectful, to not overstep boundaries.

"I think the appropriate person is the one who shows up," Ana said, "and dedicates their time and effort.

"So," she continued, courteous but pointed, "do you *want* to get involved?"

| | |
|---|---|
| *En la bella montaña* | *In the beautiful mountain* |
| *Yo vi la nieve volar,* | *I saw the snow fly,* |
| *Y sobre la nieve,* | *And on the snow,* |
| *El sol cabalgar.* | *The sun ride.* |
| *Jugaban tan felices,* | *They played blissfully* |
| *Con tanta libertad.* | *With such liberty* |
| *Y yo los envidiaba,* | *That I envied them* |
| *Deseando con tantas ganas* | *And I wished with great energy* |
| *Poder volar.* | *That I could fly.* |
| *(Jeremias's original)* | *(Ana's translation)* |

*On the lovely mountain*
*I saw snow take flight*
*And on the back of the snow*
*Watched the sun alight.*
*They played so happily*

*With such free delight.*
*That I envied them, unchained*
*While all my wishes strained*
*Toward flight.*
                    (*My translation*)

Traveling, I was aware of the tremendous freedom of movement and freedom from suspicion that my blue eyes and the pass-
port in my pocket conferred. While activist friends inside the US
decried this country for its many faults, living abroad gave me a
different perspective on the promise of America, viewed from the
outside. In other countries I'd lived, the story told was that the
US was a place where no dream was too wild, no aspiration un-
founded, a place where you could do whatever, be whatever, and
no one would kill you for it, or laugh at you, or think you were
getting above your station. In places more bounded by tradition,
there was a limit to dreams. But, the stories said, not here.

I'd benefited from this freedom to dream impossible dreams,
to sit out on the street with a typewriter and dare people to take
me seriously, to share their stories with me. Looking at Jeremias's
poems was the smallest thing I could do, but it was also a chance
to pass on the greatest gift I received from strangers at my typewriter: the gift of taking someone's words seriously.

"Jeremias calls me his representative, and everyone working
to help him he calls his team," Maria Elena told me. I knew working on Jeremias's poems would make no difference to US immigration policy or his individual legal case, but it just might make

a difference to him. I knew how it felt to go from feeling alone to having a team.

In the new year, I visited Tijuana with Maria Elena to meet Jeremias in person. We spent the day in a camp for asylum seekers, a cluster of tents hidden away between abandoned building walls in a suburb. There was a baby in the camp, ready to take its first steps, but the mother didn't dare put the baby down on the floor because of the jagged gravel shards that doubled as a bed for fifty or so migrant dreamers. A group that the US tracks as a terrorist organization was responsible for the bare luxury of the concrete walls protecting these migrants from being abused on the street, moved along, or hassled by police.

Jeremias and Maria Elena and the various people we visited joked and caught up, but their small talk was filled with bureaucratic systems and the latest news of activist movements. Finally on the outside with the power to do more than write poetry, Jeremias was a flurry of action. But I brought a copy of the book he wrote in prison, and after a day of travel and talk and food, as we were saying good-bye, I asked him to sign it. It was an artifact of a quieter, more desperate time, almost a shameful reminder. But it was also a document of survival, proof he'd made it through and lived to fight another day. Jeremias laughed and looked down at the small book of his poems, blushing and smiling. He signed it.

On the drive back up to LA from Tijuana, we got stuck behind a five-car pileup and sat in the unmoving car on the freeway for three hours. I got out and went up ahead fifty feet, past stopped lines of traffic in the dark, to see the mangled wreck. Along the way, windows started rolling down, strangers who were anonymous faces on the freeway got out of their cars to talk to one another, swapping gossip, speculating. Eventually, a few cars started bumping music and people danced, not because they were in the mood to party, but to get through this long night.

The twisted insides of the wrecked cars carpeted the highway ahead of us. Emergency crews worked to get the injured and dead out before worrying about steel and oil. Finally, the police cleared the traffic behind us, and everyone got back in their cars and turned laboriously around. We were directed by a gloved officer to an exit behind us on the freeway. And so we drove the wrong way on the 405, to look for a new route home.

Maria Elena confided in me as we drove that she had been grateful to work on poetry with Jeremias during his detention because it gave her something to do, a way to feel useful. It's hard to make friends with a stranger unless you have a reason to talk—unless you're united by a project. Maria Elena wasn't an attorney, so she couldn't work with Jeremias on legal strategy, but she could at least do this—could offer herself as witness to his humanity in dark times, to give him an open ear and a supportive but stern editor to help hone his writing. I was humbled by the scale of it, this showing up for a stranger not just for a moment but for years.

Poetry was a way to make space for the Kafkaesque absurdity of the immigration system, of the endless waiting, something to turn to when nothing else made sense anymore. Only poetry could reach that level of real-life hyperbole. But poetry could also slip between the cracks of maximum-security prisons built to isolate people.

Poetry was the tool by which two strangers who only ever met through a glass window established a shared citizenship, deeper than national citizenship. This refusal to be strangers itself, I understood, was a globally invisible but personally vital act of resistance for all the parties involved.

It made me wonder what it would look like to remove the word *stranger* from our vocabularies, to all be *something*s to each other. To call everyone we haven't met yet *friend*.

# Homecoming

*Sometimes, to make a home,*
*we have to leave—stretch—return.*
*Landing lights on the runway—*
*Tonight, no one is lost.*

California is burning. Once it was seasonal, now there are fires year-round. In LA, people do not complain about the heat, which extends deep into December and only breaks with the new year. The midwestern hopefuls do not remember when it was cooler because they are not from here, like I am. It's a city of transplants so it's always forgetting its history.

The fires make a silhouette of the skyline, ringing the city in smoke and light. This land was all desert, and it longs to return to how it was. The heat is the great leveler. It has flattened the palm trees in South Central, where I live now. It's a ramshackle shanty-town of World War II housing that's falling apart in the sun, under the glare of downtown's glass citadels. The *paletero* wades through it with his cart, selling Captain America ice creams.

I drive to my typewriter parties across LA. Not everyone in this city is dancing, but many are. Sometimes I sweat through my poetry vest and come home sunburned. Sometimes I squint through the dark at my typewriter at midnight, but at least nights are so warm here that I don't need a jacket. Everyone tells me they need a poem. Aside from their romantic partners, the main topic that young people ask me to write about is transition. Because I'm based in LA, half the people I talk to are far from home, following dreams, making new selves and new homes. But for this same reason, many are frustrated, are working against time and space and financial realities to form new identities, to become the people they want to be.

At a *La La Land*–themed party on a downtown rooftop, there's a flash mob and an essential oils lady. Appropriately for LA, we're on the top floor of a brutalist cement parking garage. But the top floor has been cleared of vehicles except the classic cars that sit catty-corner at the entrance in showroom condition, opening up on a full bar and myriad amusements, each themed (at random, as far as I could tell) after an area of town. I sit in "HOLLYWOOD" in a movie set chair typing not poems, this evening, but notecard-size scripts. The LA Tourism and Convention Board is putting on a show for out-of-town moguls, and I'm one pony in the dog and pony show.

"What genre would you like?" I ask people. "And what does your main character want?"

Two stage directions and 4–6 lines of dialogue, that's what I'm serving tonight.

A server with the catering company asks me, "Can you write me a monologue that gets me the part at any audition?"

I laugh. "I'm not that good!" I say. I'm talking about my own abilities as a writer and not hers as an actress, but even as I realize I'm accidentally insulting her my dumb mouth goes on: "I'm not a miracle worker!" I can't help feeling bad afterward. You try to be ironic and self-deprecating and end up coming across as an asshole. That's LA.

After the event, the catering company gives everyone to-go boxes. The old tiger who runs the food says, at large events, they'll call a homeless shelter to pick it up. "It's a sin to waste food!" he proclaims. That's LA too.

There's a certain solidarity with all the staff, all these people working behind the scenes to put on the big show that we're all constantly putting on here, all these actors and models and artist dreamers working in catering day in and day out, fueled by bigger dreams. All the dudes unironically call me "brother." One of the elfin serving women, still beautiful but no longer fresh faced, asks, "Will you write about us?"

The City of Angels brings in people from all over. In my work, I meet hundreds of aspiring actors from the Midwest, seeking fame and fortune in the arts. "I don't know where the confidence came from to throw my stuff in the car and move to LA. It definitely wasn't in my character before, I just did it," my friend Erica says. "Art is like mining—we're all chasing after the gold rush, following other artists to where we think the gold might be."

Erica and I met interning in an office in an LA theater. And when I say "theater" I mean converted mechanic's shop, and when

I say "office" I mean the crawl space above the lobby. During our breaks, we would experiment with our art in the theater's parking lot and on the street, trying to lure passersby in to discover the space. While I took a typewriter out, Erica would don whiteface and a fake red nose. She would take up a position on the street corner, holding a flower out to traffic on Santa Monica Boulevard, as if offering it to passing cars.

Erica had just graduated from what she called "clown college" in Northern California before moving south to LA to pursue acting. *Clown* in this case referred not to birthday party entertainment, but absurdist theater. She explained to me that clowning brokers no space for *pretending* to do something. Pretending implies that you know the thing you're trying to do is not real, that it's impossible. The clown lives so fully in the moment that everything the clown does is *real*. When Erica looked longingly at the cars with her plastic flower, she wasn't pretending for a second. She was genuinely offering a gift to the traffic.

The cars never stopped. Still she stood.

For Erica, the unsuspecting commuter audience's response was beside the point. She was laying claim to this small strip of Santa Monica Boulevard with her art, contesting the meaning of the space, challenging everyone on their way to Chipotle or hot yoga to realize there was a tiny theater run by Russians and staffed by midwestern clowns in the converted mechanic's shop at the heart of Hollywood.

I couldn't help but respect that kind of dedication to the absurd.

---

But like so many artist friends in LA, Erica struggled for two years in the city to make it before returning home—in her case, to Grand Forks, North Dakota. Big cities bring people together, but often it's just for a few years, creating communities that spread over the country as individuals get eaten up and spit out. Keeping up close connections becomes impossible, but in a digital age even the faintest acquaintances offer forays into each other's worlds, glimmers of history colliding. Our relationships fragment across physical and digital space, our friendships maintained despite missing chunks of years. LA isn't unique in this pattern of shifting communities, though it's perhaps more pronounced in a place where people come to "make it."

One afternoon, while I was still in my first year writing poetry full-time and Erica had just moved back home, she called me. "I'm hosting a spoken word night at a theater in Grand Forks," she said, getting right to the point. "Would you come up and be the featured poet?" I had never been asked to perform out of state before, let alone to be the featured poet at a show! This was it! North Dakota was going to be my big break.

Grand Forks got its name because it sits at the fork of two rivers. It had been an important trading post for the native Ojibwe with first French and later English settlers. First ox carts, then steamboats stopped there carrying supplies between Saint Paul, Minnesota, and Fort Garry, which would become Winnipeg, Canada.

On one fateful steamboat trip, the story goes, a captain and his crew found a keg of beer floating in the river and got so drunk that they had to tie up at Grand Forks for the night. While the men were sleeping, winter came. By dawn, the temperature had dropped and the river was frozen solid, locking the boat in place for the winter. The men set about building a camp to survive the subzero temperatures and wait for the ice to thaw. The crew was supplied overland through the winter, and the captain returned that spring to claim nine acres and build at the spot where the rivers met. That was the birth of Grand Forks.

When I arrive, it's summer and the grassland stretches flatly to the horizon, broken up only by big rigs, tractors, and long warehouse buildings. Grand Forks's present-day status as the third largest city in North Dakota doesn't mean it's big. With fifty thousand people and a downtown consisting of three streets, it's a small city with dreams of grandeur. Like that of most small cities across the nation, the local chamber of commerce is working to try to attract outside investment to raise property values and increase tax revenue. As cities like LA grapple with the gentrification and displacement this causes, others like Grand Forks are trying to figure out their own way to get a piece of the pie—to make development part of their narrative.

In a tried-and-true strategy borrowed from any number of urban redevelopment tools, the chamber of commerce hosts an art show called ArtSee every year in the basement of the Empire Arts Center. Most of the art in the show consists of landscapes and bright, commercial paintings that remind me of dentists' offices. Ten local artists are exhibiting their work, joined for one night in 2015 by a poet from out of town, writing custom poems on his typewriter. Me.

I'm midway through writing a poem for this sweet gray-haired lady about her new granddaughter when a surly, English voice over my left shoulder says, "Write me a poem about the fucking painting dog." I turn to see the speaker—an unkept man with a catlike face (whiskers included!) wearing paint-splattered overalls. He introduces himself as Adam Kemp, one of the other artists exhibiting at ArtSee.

The "fucking painting dog" is directly across from me. It's a small spotted dog, just bigger than a chihuahua, perched like the king of the world on a table littered with paint detritus, its owner clucking behind it. It's just being a dog, but a camera crew for the local news channel materializes and suddenly gravitates to it. For the cameras, the dog's owner dips a paintbrush covered in bite-marks in bright paint to gently place between the dog's teeth. The animal, in turn, sort of shivers against the canvas for a second, the excited bounce of a dog seeking approval. The assembled crowd, which has swelled beyond the news crew to a huddle of passersby, goes wild. The cameraman pushes through the spectators, trying to get coverage from all angles.

In Grand Forks, this is the breaking news.

The woman who owns the dog smiles masterfully and holds up a treat, at which the dog drops the brush and loses all interest in painting. The woman puts the canvas up by a dozen identical pieces in different colors on top of her table, with "for sale" signs of hundreds of dollars. All the canvases are covered in random strokes of bold color, no doubt the result of past dog-spasms. People love them, price is no obstacle.

"How can any of us compete with the fucking painting dog?" Adam mutters, gesturing at himself: a middle-aged man.

I sit in front of him, the kid from out of town, all dressed up behind my typewriter.

"Of course," he adds, slyly, "you seem to be doing all right."

I finish my poem for the grandmother and start on a poem about the painting dog for Adam, typing as the dog begins wiggling away at a new masterpiece of its own.

For Adam:

    I'd have preferred
strippers. Wouldn't you?
More honest, somehow.
    Or tigers.
If we are to call it painting
    let's have it in
       jizz or in blood
this sanitized spectacle
    of advertising as art
    tricks-for-treats as
        poetry, bears

        a bit too raw
            the work we all do.
    We are all trained
        domesticated
    pet me, feed me, give me
                love.
    I'll sit, or do the trick
        with paints for you
            over and over again.
    Originality is a scam,
    a hobgoblin. The chicken's
    still dancing! The chicken
            won't stop!


Adam swings by later in the evening to pick his poem up and laughs when I read it to him. Then, with unexpected generosity, "You should visit me in my studio while you're in town. I may have some things that need a poet later . . ."

Throughout my time in Grand Forks, I write on the typewriter for people during the day as "artist in residence" of a little hipster coffee shop unironically called Urban Stampede. Erica set the whole thing up and drops me off there in the mornings. On my first day there, who should walk in but Adam. "Come on over to my studio," he says. As it turns out, it's literally next door.

The studio is the art version of a war zone. I venture tentatively to find walking room through a maze of vandalized road signs and wooden flats splattered with layers of colorful paint. For Adam, it's a map of projects old and new, all competing for the same space. He gleefully shows me his stolen road sign series, each sheet of city-owned metal vandalized with the stencil of the fish. At first it looks like the ichthys (I had to look up the name—I just knew it as "the Jesus fish"), but Adam shoots that interpretation down. "I've been working on art for this boathouse," he tells me. "And there's an old saying—'You know the water's good as long as you can eat the fish.' If there's contamination, it shows up there first." The fish is a symbol for the health of an ecosystem, its fitness for human habitation. Adam gifts me a stolen North Dakota road sign spray-painted with one of his fish to take back to LA.

He has a series of letters between himself and the city council, arguing over the completion of and payment for an artwork—he is treating the back-and-forth writing itself as a performance, and proudly shows me his absurd responses to official letters, designed to highlight the absurdity of bureaucracy itself. "These fucking libertarians," he says cheerfully. "I just don't get it. They're all about individual freedoms and people doing what they want until you do something they don't like, and then suddenly they're all too glad to have a rulebook to throw at you. I'm a Brit and I'm constantly having to remind them, 'This is America!' People came here to get away from rules."

I find this statement prominently on display in the middle of his art studio:

FOR ALL YOU PEOPLE THAT
HAVE HAD ENOUGH OF
ENVIRONMENTALIST HYPE AND
OVERBEARING FACTUAL
STATEMENTS, HERE'S ANOTHER
ONE YOU MIGHT FIND DIFFICULT
TO SWALLOW: IN AMERICA WE
PRODUCE 12,000 TONS OF
EXCREMENT AN HOUR.

In addition to his studio, Adam has a show in an art gallery on the same block. Everything in downtown Grand Forks is on the same block. Adam's finished work seems at first to be as messy as his studio, layered graffiti-like with images ranging from realistic to cartoon, spilling off their canvases in all sorts of materials, like new thoughts supplanting old ones at the pace of a mind.

Adam's pride is the monumental canvas that takes up most of the back wall. "I've invited people to deface my artwork," he says, gesturing to a table in front of the canvas, which has a bunch of paintbrushes and markers on it. People have written everything from inspirational quotes to rude jokes, and you can tell how high on the canvas children could reach because the bottom half is full of crudely drawn dogs.

Adam adds his own layers to the collaborative painting every few days, linking everything people leave him somehow into an aesthetic unity. He makes it all look so organic and unplanned and I can't figure out for the life of me how he does it. Adam would never use the word *collaboration*, though—what he's trying to do is provoke people to *misbehave* with him. He takes the poem about the painting dog that I wrote for him and thumbtacks it right into the middle of the big canvas, punching a hole through his own painting.

"Inclusion is a political ideal," Adam says, "but it's also a physical act."

After seeing Adam's gallery, I return to Urban Stampede, where Erica picks me up. It's nice out and we walk by the riverbank. Erica tells me about the great flood, when she was a kid, that left half the town homeless. There are still signs with historical photos all up and down the riverfront, in front of the relatively recent barrier wall, chronicling the devastation in the nineties. Erica remembers the days when her school auditorium became a temporary shelter, all those displaced by the flood huddling together, drawing even closer and more tight-knit as a community.

Erica is in the thick of starting a theater company, and when not recounting history her mouth is full of nonprofit arts language. I recognize some of the language as a progression in thought from the theater where we used to work together ("curate, connect, collaborate"), but there's other stuff too, a sort of secular spirituality: "May we be conduits to the heart, always. That's my motto," Erica says. She's just started a new company called Conduit Theatre.

"Part of this is playing the religion card in a deeply religious place," Erica tells me. "I talk about art as a way to 'come in contact with the infinite'—that's as close to a personal statement of religion as I can get, but it helps religious people see the value of what I'm doing." For Erica, every worthwhile creative project has four components: effort, risk, momentum, and joy. But the thing she's hoping her spoken word event will bring, what she's seen missing in her community, is vulnerability.

Before returning home after our walk, Erica and I swing by the Empire Arts Center, where our show will be. I'm stopped dead in my tracks. They have a marquee, and it has my name on it:

THE WORD PARLOR

FEATURING LA POET

BRIAN SONIA-WALLACE

I immediately take a picture and post it to Instagram. Holy crap, I think, that's going to double my social capital right there. I'm performing in the "intimate" (read, "basement") space, but the marquee doesn't say that. As we go about our day, I periodically sneak looks at my phone to see how many "likes" the picture gets. I imagine myself getting more and more offers for performance, based on this one Instagram picture from North Dakota, my name featured progressively more prominently. Even if I don't make any money this trip, the thirst for validation has been fulfilled—and for artists, that is a big thirst.

At two o'clock in the morning the night before I perform, I find myself sandwiched between seven drunk North Dakotans in the inner sanctum of an old firehouse, where the redbrick walls have been stripped and painted black. There are no longer hoses and fire trucks here, but instead rows of empty seats on elevated risers.

Everyone is belting out *Les Misérables*. One of the drunk North Dakotans grabs me into a side bear hug. We are all sweating, gesticulating wildly into the air, voices suspiciously on key.

A stage had been installed at one end of the firehouse, and as "The Time Warp" from *Rocky Horror Picture Show* comes on the karaoke machine, the few people who were slouched in chairs rise to join in. Most of them are in their thirties and forties, though there's one older woman who's still singing with the best of us. Everyone knows all the steps to the dance, with the stage lights for an audience of no one.

Erica sits in a corner, smiling, still wearing makeup to look like an old man. During the course of my visit she's been performing in a community theater show, and these are all her fellow actors. Erica has been sober for years now, is an Alcoholics Anonymous devotee, but rises to join her drunken friends in a rendition of "Bohemian Rhapsody."

It's a song that's hard to make even more overblown, but we manage it.

The question I get over and over again in Grand Forks is, "Why are you here?" These actors don't ask that, they just press beer into my hands. This is community theater and they all have other jobs: a few teachers, an accountant. No one really talks about those lives. I get the sense that these are all the queers and misfits of Grand Forks, people who have rejected or been rejected by the mainstream of the small, tight-knit community. It clicks that they've all wound up together here at the theater, a space for exploration and play, a space where things are not already fixed. This intentional community is a place where everyone's greatest asset is their ability to chameleon themselves into what they need to be.

As the night (actually, morning) finally winds down, we are all sweaty and out of breath. The bars in Grand Forks have long since closed, all of downtown shut down for the night aside from this fire station with its lingering actors. Community theater is often cheesy and ragtag, but after the vast impersonalness of adult life in LA, this is the closest thing I've felt to really being part of a community since college.

The next night, in the basement of the Empire Arts Center for my big show, I ask the audience to snap if something I say resonates with them. We practice it before I get started, breaking the reverential silence people have been in for the open mic that preceded me. A woman had gotten up to talk about frozen tundra and tractors, followed by a man whose poetry was all directed to God. Erica had kicked the night off by lighting incense, asking everyone to shut their eyes, all "calling into the universe" for people to open their hearts and minds.

I begin my set, the tails of the Edwardian overcoat I've chosen for the occasion swishing around my heels. "Help!" one poem begins. "My internet blacked out!"

While onstage my body fights its own excitement. Time moves differently, onstage, and I dance with it, holding lines out so they linger in the air or pausing to let laughter ripple through the crowd. The stage is just a sticky patch of floor in the basement venue, with maybe a hundred people looking on from seats at tables, but the crowd is rapt—a poetry night is not something that happens every day in Grand Forks.

When I get to a section in a poem about finding out over Facebook about a college friend's suicide, there's an audible gasp. With its long, isolating winters, North Dakota has one of the highest suicide rates in the US, and it's grown almost 60 percent in the past twenty years. During the winter months, people tell me after the show, the only interaction folks will have for weeks is online. Behind the slow midwestern speech of many folks is a deep loneliness. I wonder what it's like to live in a place where the chances of meeting someone like you are so small—"Terminally unique," I call us in my poem. Here, that rings especially true.

This loneliness is by design. My next poem for the crowd is an ode equally to infrastructure and our ability to connect:

America's highways were constructed out of fear
World War II paranoia
that if we were centralized,
if we were close together, you and I,
if we could touch
and whisper each other's names into the back of one another's necks,
we would become targets.

The Germans recovered well during the war
because they had the Autobahn
so when the Allies bombed one supply line
there was always another.
So we built cities without a heart,
scattered nodes connected by veins
like jellyfish
—no brain but a neural network—
basic sensory functions
so we can move toward light and darkness
but we cannot understand what they are,
and we do not know what casts the shadow.

I took poem orders from dozens of people who'd seen me perform back to LA on slips of paper to write and mail poems in the weeks that followed my visit, meditating on each person I met. As I dropped the poems off at the post office to be mailed to North Dakota, the thought crossed my mind that these poems were a part of me that would stay in the north for winter. I am part of this community online, now, plugged in whenever the algorithm decides. In an age of social media, we never really leave a place as long as we know someone there.

Adam was older, settled. He was at the end of his migration, his concept of home fixed. The other people I met in North Dakota were closer to my age, still figuring out how to make a path in the world, how to balance work and fulfillment and comfort. Many of the folks I met during karaoke at the old firehouse are living in different parts of North Dakota themselves, now, young people leaving for jobs when work never materializes in town, while the older and more established folks stay. The tight-knit family of artists I encountered turned out to exist only for that show.

This is the blessing and curse of theater, but also of communities at large, that a community is just the configuration of people who are close at a moment in time. We can huddle together for the winter and start a city, but who makes up that city is a constantly shifting patchwork.

Grand Forks is a college town, which means it's an itinerant place, the population swelling with students in the spring and fall and dying down in the summer and winter. It's a given here that, to make something of yourself, you need to leave. There's a constant cycle of coming home and going out to add new parts to your personhood to bring back, constant reinvention of home for the selves we become.

Speaking with small-town friends about the rural-urban divide in the States, about the brain drain that inevitably happens as artists and liberals from small towns and midwestern cities set their sights on the coasts, I propose the idea of "cultural missionaries," modeled after the Evangelicals I'd seen proselytizing the Bible in South America. "Have you heard the good word?" the cultural missionaries in my vision would ask. "Look! It's art! It's poetry!"

When I visited Grand Forks for the second time, Erica had already moved away again, this time to the region's urban center in

Saint Paul, Minnesota. It was the dead of winter, and I was here for another headlining show based on her recommendation, this time for former students at the University of North Dakota at Grand Forks. Erica told me that she tried for over a year to create her own theater company here but found it impossible to generate sufficient audience or funding to sustain her work. "Grand Forks is a town that always wants the next thing but never supports the thing that's actually happening," Erica says. "At the end of the day, I had to ask myself, 'Do I have the capacity to rewrite the myth of this place?'

"When I came back from LA, I'd always hear people call artists mentally unhinged. Conservatives see art as a conspiracy theory . . . once you're an adult, it's a childish endeavor you shouldn't be engaged in. People would rather drink themselves into oblivion every night." The idea I get from Erica is that the people she grew up with saw self-discovery as a box to check by the time you're eighteen, and that after that it was time to get married, settle down, and get a house. American Dream 101.

But Erica had tried to follow the prescribed path, and it didn't work for her. She married her high school sweetheart, only to get divorced a few years later and enter a recovery program to get sober. It was around this time she discovered her love for clowning as an art form. "The clown always bounces back," Erica explains. "The clown makes us laugh and cry simultaneously." It wasn't just art for her. It was medicine.

"In LA, where everyone looks different on the street, I started picking up stuff at thrift stores that just felt good to wear," Erica says. "But coming back to Grand Forks, it suddenly felt too loud. I found myself slowly migrating back to jeans and T-shirts to fit in." Defiance seemed a lonely way to live, and Erica was searching for community. After moving home, she started working with Open Flame Theatre in the Twin Cities, a company of all queer and trans artists, and came to recognize and embrace the fact that she, herself, was trans. I only knew Erica in person in a male body, but as of this writing she has begun exclusively using female pronouns and the name Erica and asked me to use these when speaking about her past as well. "Now I dress how I want," Erica says, "and people stare. There's no coping mechanism for it, I just do it and adjust."

"Does Grand Forks still feel like home?" I ask her.

"Everywhere I've lived is home for me," Erica says. "Los Angeles is still home, as is North Dakota, and now Minnesota." I'm reminded of what Maya Angelou says: "I long, as does every human being, to be at home wherever I find myself." Adam, in his paint-splattered coveralls, told me that he makes a home for himself in his sketchbook—Erica was finding a new home in her own skin.

Home and identity seem inextricably linked to me. When people ask for a poem, the most important thing I can get from them is a setting, and the poetry becomes a meditation on place as much as personhood. Joan Didion is often quoted as saying, "The impulse for much writing is homesickness. You are trying to get back home, and in your writing you are invoking that home, so you are assuaging the homesickness."

But for myself, I never meant to come home. When I turned eighteen, I got the hell out of Culver City, where I'd grown up, an enclave of cookie-cutter veterans' housing and classic cars at the heart of LA. I fled to St Andrews, Scotland, where the breweries had been making beer longer than the US had been a democracy, and from which sallying point I would hitchhike through the Balkans and smoke hookah on the streets of Cairo. I knew no one in Scotland. It was the fresh start I craved.

I moved during the tail end of the Bush administration, and if I could have abandoned my Americanness and taken up world citizenship, I would have. My adolescence had been marked by No Child Left Behind and a state of perpetual war, and I had lived in Chile during middle school because of my dad's work, so I knew other countries were an option. When people in Scotland asked where I was from, I'd say "California" rather than "the US." My accent started to morph, vowels elongating British-ly, just enough to blur any sense of being *from* a particular place. I was young enough that I felt like because I knew no one, I could be anything and everything.

In college, I had a job showing high schoolers and their overbearing parents around my St Regulus Hall, a drafty, turreted Victorian building on the Scottish bluffs that now housed university students. My favorite story to tell them, after lies about the food, was that Saint Regulus was a fourth-century saint who was given the holy task of bearing the remains of Saint Andrew from the Vatican to "the ends of the earth." When Regulus landed under the cliffs of frigid Scotland, he said, "I've arrived."

When I graduated from university and my student visa ran out, I had no idea what was next. I kept coming back to an idea from high school history class: Manifest Destiny. How wonderful to have purpose preordained. Pack up the wagons and move to uncharted lands (of course, it didn't end well for the people already living there). Go west, young man! But I was from LA, off the coast, I'd spent my childhood at the end of Manifest Destiny, I'd done sea to shining sea. Where could I turn to for my new horizons? What was newer and tackier than LA? Vegas?

Manifest Destiny hit a limit for the settlers, the missionaries, the snake-oil salesmen and outlaws.

They ran out of land.

The American Dream is endless reinvention of self, the Capitalist Dream is endless growth. When we hit the Pacific Coast, it split the country in two. The prospect of California entering the Union, the question of whether it would be admitted as a slave or free state, led to civil war.

What happens when we can't reinvent ourselves anymore? When we can't drop everything and move west? When we ran out of land, we urbanized, a new frontier in technology, everything constantly better and faster, railroad tracks and belching factories becoming rockets and the first man on the moon. The early internet felt like a pioneer town, anonymous chat rooms like Old West saloons at dial-up speed. But we are moving to a space where even digitally we are running up against the limits of self-reinvention with the social internet, eternal recording and surveillance that demands consistency to brand. So what's next?

Do we move backward?

*Mad Men*'s Don Draper says, "There is no such thing as American history, only a frontier." But what if that frontier is the past, at long last, a hard reckoning we've been putting off? As progress sweeps us all along more and more quickly, suddenly the past and the present start to coexist, the typewriter and the iPhone, the train and the airplane. What it means to be American is shifting, so fast that generations are mutually unintelligible to each other in the pace of our lives, the content of our desires, the quality of our connections. What's being repeated, between places and generations? What's being replaced?

If I travel my native country speaking to everyone, one person at a time, it is because I am still trying to find myself here.

I am still trying to make this place home.

# After the Fire

The sun reflects brilliantly off the waves of the Pacific, throwing shadows on the charred hills where tufts of green are just starting to emerge from blackened soil. Perry Como's "(There's No Place Like) Home for the Holidays" plays on the radio.

The last embers from the Woolsey Fire—the destructive wildfire that burned close to one hundred thousand acres in the course of a few days in November 2018 in LA and Ventura counties—have finished their march to the sea, and now former residents are starting to return and grapple with rebuilding their lives. Rick Mullen, the mayor of Malibu, likened the area to a post-apocalyptic landscape, comparing the energy released during the devastation to being "nuclear in scale." In contrast to the leveling of Paradise in Northern California by fire, the Malibu I see is a surreal patchwork of suburban properties with only minor scorch marks that have been decked out with holiday cheer, next to charred lots, as if meteors had struck every third house.

Two weeks earlier, I drove up to write poetry at a bridal shower just a few miles from the fire, teetering the whole time on the edge of evacuation. Ash rained down around my car as I crossed the mountains on the 405, and even though all my windows were rolled up I started coughing. The wedding I was writing at that evening was moved, on the same day, because the venue that was supposed to house it was burning.

The poems I wrote that day took on a sharp edge, and people told me not just about their loves, but about their relationships that were frayed and needed mending. Writing for one woman about her anxieties around family during the holidays, I remembered Pompeii, the city frozen forever in one moment by ash.

They dug under the city,
found columns rising
from just beneath
the basement,
a quiet residential
neighborhood of fragments
that had lasted centuries.

We, too, build our houses
with stones from the temple,
pattern mosaics from wine-stained amphorae
split in centuries-old-wars,
stand hurting and laughing
on history.

You have painted your face
with ashes and glitter

for the holidays.
Sparkling, you tender
sea glass between your fingers,
finding the perfect fit
for edges worn smooth,
sand blasted transparent.
Longing to become whole again
in new configurations.

Coming back to Malibu after the fires I am a different person—not a poet here to commemorate love lives, but a journalist on assignment for *Rolling Stone* to try to figure out how people are rebuilding. A year earlier, I'd chatted with a journalist who did typewriter poetry on the side about how the skills both practices used were the same: talking to people and getting them to open up. Now I'd have to put that theory to the test.

"If you get there a little early, feel free to walk around," Erin Shirk texts. She's arranged for me to meet her grandparents, Jim and Marcella Shirk, on a Sunday afternoon at what was left of their home on Kanan Dume Road in Malibu. Just a fragment of the house's blue wooden fence still stands, leaving the guts of the property in full view of the neighborhood: a few brick columns, rubble that's been moved into neat piles, and a burnt-out Ford Model A from the 1920s.

A dozen neighbors and family members gather and mingle with the Shirk grandparents while I talk about their rebuilding a week before Christmas. One brings out a wooden sign, like a theatrical backdrop, painted with the words "Happy 92 Papa Jim." On November 6—two days before the fires ignited and consumed this house and destroyed 1,643 structures and damaged 364 others in two counties—Jim turned ninety-two. The nonagenarian's story is like many others in this aging community affected by the blaze: they are determined to rebuild their houses as they were, though they may not live to see construction completed.

The elderly couple are both dressed for the holidays—Marcella wears earrings shaped like bells and a pin of a cat in a Santa hat. "It has been one miracle after another," she says. They're thankful for a GoFundMe page their granddaughter Sarah set up in the aftermath of the fire to help with reconstruction costs for her fixed-income grandparents. The fundraising page surpassed its goal to raise $10,730 in a month with 156 donations from around the world, with over 90 percent of the donations being one hundred dollars or less.

Kindness from strangers was a recurring theme in Marcella's stories about the fire, from a stranger in the next booth at IHOP who picked up their tab without a word the morning after they were evacuated, to a health insurance representative on the phone who found a loophole in the rules to replace a sleep apnea machine and invited the couple to her house for Thanksgiving dinner if they had nowhere to go. "We are very, very strong believers," Marcella says. "God has been good to us."

"We moved in here in 1977," she explains. "It was the cheapest land in LA County. Over half of us here [in Malibu] are old-timers, plain old folks like us." Marcella had a career in sales for various pet food companies, while Jim was a bricklayer. When the couple moved onto the property, they lived with two teenagers in a one-bedroom shed, gradually building out over the years into a family complex made up of two houses and a mobile home on an acre of land.

The house at the top of the hill and the mobile home burned, and years of memories and sentimental objects with them; Jim jokes that his family was always trying to get him to get rid of stuff. The house at the bottom of the hill, where the couple's starter shed once stood, survived. They gave me oranges to take home from the trees around it. The Shirks are planning on spending Christmas Eve at this surviving house, where two of their adult children now live.

"We've gone through a few fires," Marcella says. "The fence has gone up twice in smoke—the next one is going to be cement!" This couple has seen their share of suffering and seem resolute in the face of this latest loss. Jim grew up during the depression in small-town Indiana, and fought for the Navy during World War II, where he was wounded on D-Day on the beach in Normandy. Meanwhile, Marcella was born in Czechoslovakia, and her family escaped first to Singapore and then, when the Japanese invaded, to Australia. "We were part of a convoy of three ships," she explains, "and the other two were torpedoed." From Australia, Marcella came to America to study art. "I immigrated the *right* way," she tells me, and I carefully (though guiltily) skirt the topic—Fox News talking points aren't part of the feel-good story I'm trying to tell. I change the subject to how the couple's romance started, back when Marcella was a student.

"We've been married for sixty-two years," Jim says, with a twinkle in his eye. "If you can survive that . . ." They both laugh.

Marcella and Jim hail their neighbor as a hero, and bring him over to talk, despite his objections. He owned his own fire-fighting gear and hose, and when the water stopped working during the fires, he used a pump to get water from his pool to fight the flames. He's a Hollywood producer, he explains, and managed to save most of the livestock on his land, including one of the llamas featured in the movie *Water for Elephants*.

In contrast, Marcella fumes about the city's response, both during and after the fire. "In the old days, we had help," she says, telling me that she saw fire trucks sitting at the bottom of the hill while their home burned. Her granddaughter claims that they called the city first, then the fire department, to no avail, before finally calling ABC7—the nightly news. Jim and Marcella may have moved into Malibu as "plain old folks," but you don't live around the corner from Hollywood for that long without learning that sometimes the quickest way to get something done is to be on TV.

The Kanan Dume Road property was a family compound, and a portrait quickly emerged of a family who knows the importance of telling their story and telling it well. From the GoFundMe page to an ABC7 interview, and the family's willingness to stage a mini-reunion just to speak with this writer, the Shirks weren't going to let the fire stop them from crafting their own narrative, making sense of this tragedy by telling its story themselves. Marcella shared her worries about dealing with the city in rebuilding, telling me that she's heard horror stories of people not being allowed to reconstruct their homes where they were.

So far, despite skeptical ecologists and historians who warn that the natural ecology of the southern California hills includes inevitable destructive fires every twenty years or so, local government agencies have responded to the Woolsey Fire by relaxing rules so residents could rebuild their properties exactly as they had been. Ironically, some of the regulations going by the wayside to grandfather in rebuilt homes are updated fire safety standards. Other regulations have been relaxed to allow residents who have been living with family, friends, and in hotels since the fire to return to their properties and live in trailers. "We are planning to pull a mobile home on-site to live in while we build," Marcella says.

The Shirks have both the plans and means for rebuilding, but for many other older adults, the legal and financial obstacles are too great, and they don't know what will come next. Billy Green Bush was a character actor on everything from *M\*A\*S\*H* to *The Dukes of Hazzard*, but the eighty-four-year-old divorced retiree didn't have homeowners insurance when the house he'd built decades ago burned down. He's still having trouble qualifying for FEMA assistance, which is capped at only $34,900, because one of his adult children is also on the lease. Bush told me he doesn't have the stamina to rebuild himself and he doesn't trust anyone else to build to his standards. He's been living in his 1957 Dodge van since the fire with his dog, and the van was having trouble starting when we spoke. But even in these circumstances, his fire story slid easily into evangelism when asked about his plans for the holidays. "You should give thanks every minute of every day," he said. "I'm a Jehovah's Witness, and every day is Christmas for me." It made me think of Marcella Shirk's unshakable faith and her earrings shaped like bells.

Pondering what it means to make new life from the ashes, I asked former California poet laureate Dana Gioia, who took in a family of five strangers in the wake of the 2017 Tubbs Fire, for a poem recommendation. He offered Sonia Greenfield's "Ghost Ship," written after the titular Oakland warehouse venue burned. The poem ends:

> But you can't live in fear of the apparition . . .
> It can happen any time to anyone . . .
> you have to dance
> as if the very act of living depends on it.

After the story came out, Billy Bush's son found my email address and sent whole paragraphs of his family's story with dramatic photos of the property on fire, and a link to the GoFundMe he'd just launched to buy his dad an RV to live in on the burnt property. "There's so much more to this story . . ." he wrote.

But by then, the *Rolling Stone* article had run, and all I could do was wish him well and donate a few bucks to the fundraising efforts. I'd keep getting emails, every few weeks, updating me on the family's progress. But I could only tell that story once. The next chapter, they'd have to write themselves.

# Mic or Church?

*I ask the room to be raw*
*and the room answers. We sing together*
*but do not call it home.*

On an unremarkable Wednesday afternoon back in LA (in which season, who knows, who cares, it's always bright and hot), an earnest poetry bro friend texts me to see if I have plans that night. He's a Filipino American rapper from New York who's been hitting every open mic and befriending all the poets and auditioning as an actor and a voice actor and working a food service catering gig to make it all happen—in other words, your typical art-hustling Angeleno. He invites me to come with him to something called "Our Mic | Phase 3 | Manifest."

"It's my home," he tells me. I roll my eyes a bit at the word *manifest* in the title, but it's been a long time since I've gone and been part of that poetry scene—young, hip, and full of LA artist types, mostly people of color.

*things are about to get really real*, the Facebook event promises.

But also, *everybody is eligible. everybody is counted. everybody is invited.*

Nothing is capitalized in the event description, just to be cool. I decide to go at the last minute. I arrive late. That's kinda my MO.

The mic is on the top floor of a warehouse space deep in Skid Row, and I arrive as the performers are taking the stage. Apparently the hosts have asked people to open with their favorite memory of Our Mic, because it's an anniversary. "It gives me food for the rest of the week," says one poet. Another tells the story of how he stopped going to church when a breakup made it weird and he missed the community. But now, he tells the crowd, "you guys are my church family."

This space is all "I am" poems, detailing the poet's oppression or sadness or anger, then their self-doubt, then their realization that they are enough just as they are, and ultimately their performative self-actualization. "When I first performed, I realized a healing I didn't know I needed, and talked about an incident I'd never talked about, on the mic," one poet shares earnestly. But however sincere the stories, the mic is still an open mic which means anyone can go up, which means the quality of poetry is really uneven. It gives the whole thing the feel of a high school play, amplified by the audience's response, which is as consistent as the poetry is inconsistent. The whole crowd whoops and hollers for each person who comes up to the mic, shouting in-jokes, and however good or bad the piece, the level of applause at the end always feels . . . parental.

"This is . . . just my family! And literally everything is great!" says a poet who can't come up with a specific memory about the mic. Yes, I think, this is a space where everyone has agreed, on entry, that literally everything is great. The poets are joined by comedians and singers who all say that this is their family. They coax first-timers to get up. "This is my first time here, and I'm scared," one first-timer admits. The admission of fear elicits whoops and applause.

Lady Basco, one of the hosts, urges the poets to "go in" before they read, to commit fully to the work they're sharing. I find myself, as an audience member, holding back. I am naturally kind of grumpy and critical in art spaces, I realize, I want them to work to win me over. Sometimes I can let go and just let art be church, but often it just reminds me that I'm an atheist. A guitar player comes up to the stage to sing Leonard Cohen's "Hallelujah," as if there was a law that every open mic must feature one endless rendition of Leonard Cohen's "Hallelujah" or it doesn't count.

"My name means the Chosen One!" shouts a Korean American poet with gorgeously coiffed hair and a smart sports coat on, railing against white people who won't learn his name.

The Chosen One. Prince. Goddess. These are titles that these young, struggling poets of color try on, one after another, and the open mic becomes a place for Hollywood's caterers and grips to be rock stars. It's a drag show in words, *Paris Is Burning* 2017, and the dispossessed and hipsters alike line up to proclaim themselves amazing on some fundamental level that's immune to the wounds of oppression experienced every day.

After a woman's poem, Lady Basco tells her, "That was prob-ably the most honest thing you've ever done in this space." Sud-denly I see where this room places value, and it all makes sense. They aren't looking at the best writing or performance, but the most honesty. I wonder briefly how honesty can be quantified, whether some people's honesty can be "more genuine" than the honesty of others. I find myself cataloging honesty as a perfor-mance metric, going back through my poems and grading myself.

Beau Sia, the other host, says something that I like. Beau says, "Here, this [time at the mic] is a fraction of your existence. We use this to build the rest of our lives." I'm reminded of a quote from Brazilian political theater maker Augusto Boal, who said that the-ater is "rehearsal for the revolution." What happens onstage is set off, separate, in some ways, from everyday life, which is part of what allows people to be revelatory about their most intimate struggles and doubts. But, by airing these unspeakables onstage, the poet realizes that they can be spoken, and so cuts a chink in the taboos of everyday life. The research question being poked at is, "What if you could be totally honest?" That's the revolution these spoken word artists are rehearsing for.

That's the spell of open mics, at their best.

But we're not done yet. Lady Basco opens the second half with something I've never seen at a mic before. She calls a few perform-ers up at a time and starts directing, having them read to each other, or read something else entirely, or build collaborative pieces from what they shared earlier. When Lady Basco starts directing,

I stop writing. As unexceptional as individual pieces might have been, before, suddenly it's real and spontaneous and vulnerable.

I can't miss a moment.

Musicians join poets. Two young men, with poems about their dads, read their poems to each other as a conversation. In the end, Lady Basco makes everyone get onstage and sing a line of their poem to try to make music—that one doesn't quite work, this time, but I see how it could.

For maybe twenty or thirty minutes, I can't look away. It doesn't matter that the work onstage still swings from cringeworthy to moving and back. What I'm watching is the act of creation itself, well-curated to make sure no one is allowed to bore us. It's breathtaking.

The evening starts wrapping up, with the hosts making announcements. Beau has us stand and take a deep breath together. The breath I've seen before, and while the standing seems churchy, it's nice to get back into my body. As we take the breath, I realize the importance of this evening for me—the first time I've been in communion with other poets since I got back to LA from my travels.

Beau and Lady Basco share their own favorite moments.

"It's seen me beyond my comfort for the sake of my fulfillment," Beau says.

"It's about healing, it's about being of service, it's not about me," Lady Basco says.

Then, things take a turn for the decidedly weird.

- - -

Beau says he's "going to get a little bit psychic," and searches through the audience to pull someone up onstage—a mumbling Asian American Brooklyn rapper who performed early on and wears his awkward and his cool at the same time, like stripes and checkers. His piece was about his mother's expectations of him and the pain of pursuing music over his family's objections. Lady Basco sits him down and testifies to him, like in a for-real church way. Sermonizes, chastises him to follow his dreams, take his own path.

"The most generous thing you can do," she says, "is put your own gas mask on before someone else's." She repeats it, twice.

The guy is uncomfortable, then attentive, then tearful, then uncomfortable again. It's a come-to-Jesus moment, but the admonition is to keep making art. I thought it couldn't get more religious if it tried, but I was wrong. Suddenly, the entire congregation, and that's what we are now, bursts out singing! It's this "Believe in Yourself" song, which everyone knows by heart. It seems like maybe the song had been written just for this moment in the show—it balances out its feel-good lines with quips like "just kick your own ass" and feels distinctly homemade.

Manifest. Hallelujah. I guess the clues had been there all along. I found out later that Our Mic grew out of an association for Asian Americans working in the arts, fighting Hollywood whitewashing. It was both an advocacy group and a mutual support group for its members. The commandment to follow your passion and "do you" followed the template of standard corporate motivational speaking, though here it was in service of social justice and mixed with pan-Asian Evangelical Christianity and prosperity gospel.

This was the first time I'd seen this religious-corporate creed at a poetry space. I guess I knew that tons of LA's actors and artists subscribed to the "everything happens for a reason" and "have you read *The Art of the Deal*" and "I'm just praying God will make me famous" camps. I just hadn't quite processed that was part of who was here, until that moment. This wasn't just an open mic, it was a poetry job seminar and power of positive thinking retreat.

When the group sing finally ended (and it was not a short song), everyone fellowshipped! I mean, networked! I mean, talked!

I wasn't sure which it was anymore.

I always joked about evangelizing culture, the Poetry Crusade. But these people were doing it for real, they had started their church and it was every Wednesday night and *everybody is eligible. everybody is counted. everybody is invited. things are about to get really real.*

# The Word

Evangelical: *from the Greek* eu-angelos, *"messengers (angels) of good news."*

The American frontier evokes images of cowboys and mining towns, settlers warring with native people, gunfights and lawmen remolding the social order to their image. But before the cattle ranchers, across the plains came the missionaries. Spurred by the Second Great Awakening, missionaries believed it was their duty to remedy a corrupt society and save the unconverted before the imminent second coming of Christ. They established churches with their unique strain of American Evangelical Protestantism, in some cases even helping native people keep their land sovereign against the advances of European settlers with their gambling and drinking. The missionaries had grander designs, not in this world, but in the next.

They wanted native people's souls.

As the American frontier became a known quantity, missionaries set their sights on foreign shores. By 1900, all the major denominations had formed their own missionary societies, and there were between four thousand and five thousand American missionaries abroad trying to contact "unreached" peoples on islands and in jungles around the world. Today, there are close to forty thousand American missionaries worldwide. The missionaries brought their own beliefs about the supremacy of their ideas and culture, but in living with native people also found unlikely common ground in their suspicion of, and fight against, the corrupting influence of outside "civilization."

As I travel the US evangelizing poetry, finding solidarity and recording aspirations, I can't help but remember my first brush with American Evangelicals, six thousand miles south of American soil.

The year was 2012, before I ever touched a typewriter. I was floundering, fresh out of college in a brave new post-recession world. My friend Victor, an anthropology PhD I knew from college, invited me to the Amazon rainforest. It had been a childhood dream. And I had nowhere else to go.

Four hours from the nearest city in the heart of the Ecuadorian jungle, the bus just stopped in the middle of a gravel track. Up ahead I could see construction on the road in progress, but from here we would have to walk to get to the mission and adjoining town of Makuma. Victor led the way down a narrow path. We veered off the gravel road and into the trees, where a pair of men on horses passed us. As they stepped off the gravel, the animals sank up to their knees in deep, red mud.

Victor had been in Ecuador for six months already when I

arrived. It had taken him most of that time just to get the proper permission from the indigenous leadership to come to Makuma. Once he finally gained access, he faced the classic anthropologist's dilemma. To be in this community, to be able to spend time with local people and talk to them, he had to have something to offer. He asked me if I'd be willing to teach a theater workshop series with him, continuing the work he knew from me in college, making environmentalist political theater. I'd live with him in the spare room of the mission house he was renting and make art with people beyond the reach of paved roads.

"The Shuar were infamous in the early 1900s for wearing the shrunken heads of their enemies as magical totems," Victor told me with an anthropological glee when we first discussed me coming out. "People still die all the time in the jungle!" He was always a little morbid.

And I was here to be his offering to the Shuar.

"It used to be much worse," Victor said as we followed the horses, on foot, into the mud. "The paved road is much further along now. Soon it will reach Makuma."

Over the soupy ground, local people had laid small logs like bridges. They were narrow and simultaneously sank and rolled as I walked on them, and with every misstep my leg would plunge down to the knee in mud, so that it sloshed over the sides of my tall rain boots and squelched around my toes. We hopped from log to log for half an hour, balancing with huge backpacks in which were stuffed all of the worldly possessions we'd have for the month.

At last, the footpath opened onto a wide field. "This is the mission's airstrip," Victor explained. When the mission was established there was no road nearby, and the missionaries cleared a landing strip in the middle of the jungle to come and go using a small biplane. The remains of a rusted-out airplane from a crash still sat to one side of the landing strip, a grisly reminder of the limits of technology.

The mission was on one side of the airstrip, and on the other was the small town of Makuma. Over the years, Shuar families had flocked to build houses near the airstrip to take advantage of this one lifeline to the fruits of the industrialized world, as well as the infrastructure that the missionaries used airplanes to bring in: a hydroelectric dam and a radio station. The missionaries were thrilled—their flock was coming to them.

At 4 A.M., my alarm went off. I swung out of my too-small cot bed in the pitch black to pull on shorts and a T-shirt and stumbled out the front door, the mosquito screen banging shut behind me. The outside air was already humid, laden with the smell of wet leaves and the sound of insects. The jungle was waking up.

When my legs hit the tall grass they were instantly soaked up to the knee in dew. The rain that had been a gentle patter turned to a torrent out of nowhere, and I cursed that I'd already gotten out of bed. Picking up my pace, I sprinted across the lawn that separated our small mission house from the big house at the edge of the constantly encroaching trees. The big house had a porch out front, impenetrably dark in the predawn.

You would never know someone was sitting there until he spoke.

"You made it."

The man was tall, white, and gaunt, with a scraggly beard that made him look like a survivalist. Which, in some ways, he was. He went by Tukup, the name given to him by the indigenous Achuar people which means "good hunter," and had used only that name in the jungle for almost thirty years. He had the weathered face and arms of a man who spent most of his time outdoors and wore boots and blue jeans. Tukup had lived in the Amazon for longer than I'd been alive.

I arrived in time to see Tukup add the large and brittle dried leaves of the guayusa plant to the huge vat of boiled water sitting on the porch in front of him like a cauldron. "I'm out on my porch every morning for tea at sunrise," Tukup had told me when I arrived at the mission. "Join me any time." Not being a morning person, it took me a couple tries waking up before I made it. Tukup ladled my tea into a cup and motioned for me to take a seat beside him.

We sat on the porch for at least an hour, mostly talking about the one thing Tukup was desperate for more than anything in the world: American action movies. He was really into *Die Hard* and was just so glad to have someone to talk to about Bruce Willis. As Tukup recounted action set pieces, dawn broke, a light bursting through the mist and jungle rain.

After many cups of tea, as our conversation wound down, Tukup made his way to the edge of the porch, leaned out over the railing, and vomited.

"Are you okay?" I asked, alarmed.

"Guayusa is supposed to make you throw up," Tukup explained, eyeing the bushes that had borne the brunt of his hurling before turning back to me. "I picked it up during my time with the Achuar, who live deeper in the Amazon. They drink it every morning."

I joined Tukup at the rail, and as soon as I stood up my stomach started to roil. I had been told about guayusa, but I hadn't really believed it. Now, as the birds sang and the jungle came alive, I tightened my stomach and tensed my throat to make myself wretch. I had nothing in my stomach but the tea, which found a new home in the bushes. I felt lighter in my body but also weak, buzzing with the tea's strong caffeine.

Like the Achuar, Tukup drank the guayusa tea to vomit as part of his daily morning routine. Tukup would travel with the Achuar for weeks at a time, witnessing to people living so deep in the forest that the only way to get there was by foot. Vomiting had a practical use there, because refrigeration and preservatives were virtually nonexistent and food poisoning or parasites were primary reasons people got sick. But vomiting in the Amazon wasn't just part of a healthcare regimen, it was also central to ritual and spiritual life.

Lately ayahuasca, a potent hallucinogen that's native to the same region, has gotten popular among rich Americans seeking spiritual enlightenment. They pay thousands of dollars to come to Ecuador or Peru in order to vomit and see visions for days under the guidance (and chemical dosing) of self-proclaimed indigenous shamans. Guayusa, which Tukup made his tea from, is no ayahuasca, but its very mild psychoactive effects mean it does get used to help interpret dreams.

But Tukup was no shaman, he was an Evangelical missionary. American Evangelical missionaries had been in this region of the Amazon since the turn of the century, but they'd always been driven off or killed until this mission was established in the 1940s. Tukup was part of a long line of Americans here trying to tell the good news of Jesus Christ to "uncontacted" souls in the jungle. In a predominantly Catholic country, it was a subversive act—could the missionaries reach the native people before the state got to them?

The advent of the Evangelical Church preceded the American Revolution by just a few decades. The spirit of revivalism had an American sort of individualism and inclusivity to it, empowering ordinary men and women to share the gospel and convert others outside of the church walls. The Evangelicals would meet in private homes as small groups, divided by age and gender, to fellowship (which they use as a verb) and to study the Bible. Preachers emphasized a personal relationship with God over ritual and tradition, and missionaries to convert new souls could come from any one of the faithful.

Tukup and his wife, Lois, were farmers in Iowa "when the Lord decided to send us to Ecuador." Without the trappings of the church to rely on, preachers and missionaries alike had to rely on their charisma and oratory prowess to help their congregations get a glimpse of transcendence. Storytelling blossomed, not just biblical stories but stories of redemption as ordinary people— just like you and me—found Jesus and had their lives irreversibly changed. With the advent of media, televangelists spreading The Word as immutable and supreme blossomed over TV and radio.

Far from state infrastructure, one of the missionaries' first actions when they arrived in the Amazon was to establish a local radio station with religious programming so the far-flung Shuar families could worship in their own communities. The radio was now run by the Shuar and had expanded beyond the Bible into news and more. In a community without roads, the crackling voices on the radio bound the community together into a common narrative.

Seventy years after the mission was built, the town had grown into the biggest in the region, and the seat of the local Shuar government. The Shuar actually had two separate governments presiding over different areas, split by religion: there was a Catholic Shuar government and an Evangelical Shuar government. The missionaries had helped the Shuar in this region to organize to resist expansion by the Ecuadorian state—and the Catholicism they feared it would bring. Ecuador was a Catholic state, settled by the Spanish, and the American Evangelicals feared indigenous assimilation into the broader culture would also mean accepting all the Catholic ritual and hierarchy they found unbiblical and therefore abhorrent.

Makuma, the capital of Evangelical Shuar territory, consisted of a few dozen houses, a church, a soccer field, and a school around a single road. Some houses acted as ad hoc shops, selling rice and eggs and not much else from their windows, while one had a lunch counter where you could sit and eat while kids and chickens played at your feet.

But even as the town of Makuma thrived, the mission that had helped start it faltered. Now only two aging couples, including Tukup and his wife, still lived in the complex to spread The Word. There were more houses on the mission than families to fill them, which is why Victor and I were able to stay. Tukup told me that they existed in the Amazon "by grace," which meant Evangelical churches around the US would take collections for them to send small living stipends. "There are several churches that would consider themselves our home church," he told me. The missionaries' kids mostly lived in the US, and the missionaries would save up the little money they got to go visit every few years.

Victor gave me a new framework to use in thinking about the missionaries. "There's a temptation for us to believe indigenous communities are corrupted or destroyed by introducing Christianity and Western technology, but that's only part of the picture," Victor told me. "To say these things destroy communities is to deny that those communities themselves have agency—they are not just being acted on, they are also acting.

"I've been playing with a different metaphor. This is an agricultural area, and I like to think that the Shuar are *domesticating* Western technology to serve them, the same way they have with dangerous plants and animals in the jungle. They could have run the missionaries off at any point, but they allow them to stay. In fact, in the history of the mission, the Shuar have fed them and helped them to survive. The missionaries don't have the power here. All of us, as outsiders, are relatively weak and useless in the Amazon. If we are tolerated, it's because we are useful."

This mission had been evangelizing this same spot for over sixty years, and Tukup was frustrated by what he called "backsliding." One day he'd see Shuar converts in church, and the next he'd see them drinking chicha, the fermented yucca mash that doubled as beer and bread here. For Tukup, an essential part of accepting Jesus as your personal lord and savior was giving up alcohol.

"I was a lost drunk before I was saved," he told me, repeating almost verbatim the sort-of religious AA storyline that was central to the plot of all the Evangelical literature I found in the mission house and read to pass the long nights. But chicha wasn't just booze for the Shuar, the thick alcoholic soup was calorie-dense in an area without much nutrition, and therefore vitally important for people to have the strength to work in harsh jungle conditions. The Evangelical ask was more than accepting Jesus. It was about changing what went into sustaining native people's bodies.

The great irony for me was that the other missionaries did not partake in Tukup's guayusa tea—I wondered what they thought of his propensity to throw up and fantasize about *Die Hard* in the morning. The missionaries hadn't been able to make the locals as Christian as they'd like, but being here had perhaps made Tukup more like the Shuar than he'd admit.

I asked Tukup what he thought of the local shamans, expecting him to dismiss their beliefs as unchristian superstition. I couldn't have been more wrong. "I've seen some things you wouldn't believe," he told me. "People here tamper with black magic, and it leaves them open to *outside influences.*

"The devil is strong here. That's why it's important that the missionaries are here too."

Far from being a skeptic about indigenous magic, Tukup was fully convinced that he was caught in the middle of a constant, supernatural battle. This battle went beyond national borders, but always managed to be America-centric. "Obama is clearly the Antichrist," he told me one day, with something approaching glee. The coming of the Antichrist was one of the signs that the end of days was nigh, and Tukup was almost impatient for it to arrive. This was, after all, what the whole Evangelical movement was preparing for. He'd been in the Amazon for decades, saving souls. It was a lonely life wherein he'd leave his wife for weeks to trek through the jungle, searching for people who had yet to hear The Word.

He was ready for the world to end.

After vomiting tea with Tukup in the morning, I woke Victor up and we braved the mud into Makuma together. We made our way to the building next to the *espacio cubierto* that served as the area's community room and government office, a cavernous square of stucco with tall grass threatening to reclaim it for the jungle. We brought with us a liter of Coca-Cola that we'd bought from one of the house-window shops to bring to the young Shuar men and women, who walked for up to an hour from their home communities to meet us there.

The Shuar president "presented" me at this first meeting, to let people know I was not a spy or an oil prospector.

"It seems very formal," I whispered to Victor.

"He wants to make sure people know not to kill you," Victor said helpfully, less than half joking.

The participants in my workshops were a mix of teenagers and young adults, all part of a leadership program put together by the local government. They were mostly thrilled just to be away from their family homes and around people their own age. I led them through a warm-up and introduced the idea of theatrical conflict with a chair. One actor had a chair and had to hold on to it, the other actor had to get it from them without physically wrestling it from their hands. Scenes of persuasion, subterfuge, threats, and barter emerged.

I had recently discovered Augusto Boal's *Theatre of the Oppressed*, and it was my bible for the theater classes I taught in the Amazon. The book chronicles theater techniques for social change that Boal first developed during the Brazilian dictatorship in the 1960s, working with rural farmers, and over two months of workshops I explored almost all of his exercises with my students.

The best way to explain how Boal changed theater is through parables, which come to me from working with practitioners in his tradition through the Center for Theater and Pedagogy of the Oppressed.

During the Brazilian dictatorship, Boal's theater company arrived in a community in advance of government soldiers and performed a rabble-rousing play. They told the local people to have heart and stay strong in resisting the military. After the performance, the locals were so moved by the actors' passion for the cause that they invited them to come fight the government alongside them, to die alongside them, the next day.

"No," an embarrassed Boal explained, "our guns are fake."

The locals responded, "We have extra guns you can borrow. Come fight with us!"

"We would be useless to you," a humiliated Boal conceded. "We are only actors."

This is how Boal's modern-day disciples tell the story.

It was the beginning of a new chapter for Boal. His well-intentioned political calls to arms had backfired, and he realized that he was in no position, as an educated city kid, to tell rural farmers what was best for them. The best he could do was offer his skills as an artist and open up the theater as a platform for communities to discuss and tackle their problems themselves. To accomplish this, Boal started making plays that didn't offer a resolution, just presented a problem, and asked the audience to propose solutions for the actors to try out, ending not with a satisfying resolution but with many possible branching pathways.

But even that was not enough. Boal was showing a play where

a husband and wife had a conflict. At the crisis point, he stopped the play and asked the audience what they wanted the actors to do. One woman said the wife onstage should "speak with her husband forcefully."

The actress onstage planted her feet and got firm in her argument.

"No," the woman from the audience said, "she should speak with him *forcefully.*"

The actress onstage shouted and raged.

"Not like that!" the woman from the audience said. "Like this!"

And she took the stage, pulling off her shoe and beating the actor playing the husband out of the house. When she had finished, she put her shoe back on and took a seat. "*That's* how you speak forcefully."

From that point on, Boal would invite the audience to get up onstage with the actors and try their solutions themselves, suspicious of the divide between words and meaning for different people. But, he realized, the effect was something more—suddenly, people who had come to his performances felt empowered to take action in real life, because they had already practiced taking action onstage. They stood up to corrupt police or left abusive relationships. And Boal hadn't told them what he thought was the right thing to do, he had just created space for them to consider it themselves and practice how they might act. In his seminal text *Theatre of the Oppressed*, Boal says, "The theater itself is not revolutionary. It is a rehearsal for the revolution."

When I found Boal in college, I was an instant convert. I was studying Sustainable Development, learning about ecological crisis and policy and the million factors that need to align to change systems. Art seemed something removed, something that could never have an impact on the real world. In Boal, I found a model for an art practice that felt like it could have made a difference in the real world.

I'd be lying if I said I wasn't full of myself, as only a twenty-two-year-old fresh from college can be. When I first arrived, I had lofty and naïve dreams of my theater as a political force in the Amazon, but the real reason I was there was much simpler. The Shuar leaders I spoke with told me about a pandemic of shame and shyness in their youth, a first generation connected to the outside world and aware of their otherness and isolation from an early age. For the Shuar, having a big voice meant strength, and so the shame young people felt was robbing the next generation of their power.

I was there to help my students find their words.

My actors had their first big performance for an audience of hundreds, who walked from communities near and far for a political rally. We were in the *espacio cubierto*, which literally translates to "covered space," a concrete slab protected by a metal awning. It mostly acted as the town soccer field, and every weekend families would come together to play soccer and hold an ad hoc farmers' market. Sometimes, in the evenings, there'd be dancing, in which young eligible men and women from all the surrounding communities would stand board-straight, barely touching, and shuffle around in a colonial two-step that was both hyper-erotic and hyper-aware that the eyes of the whole community were watching.

But today, Makuma's *espacio cubierto* was playing host to a long-shot national presidential candidate, running on the indigenous party platform. All of the Evangelical area's Shuar leadership were there, and my actors were nervous and excited to get to speak. Just before my students were announced to come onstage, I watched one of them get out a bottle of green juice and pass it around. One by one, each student tipped the bottle back into their nose, snorted, and looked up sniffing and red-eyed.

"What is that?" I asked one of the actors in Spanish.

"It's tobacco juice," he explained. "It makes you brave and helps you speak."

Sure enough, onstage, the students' voices were strong. In a mix of Spanish and Shuar, they told the story of oil prospecting in the region. Makuma was in the midst of a transformation, as the road from the outside grew ever nearer, and with it the threat of national control and oil exploitation removing people from their lands. The scene my students made ended with the Shuar driving prospectors out and reasserting indigenous sovereignty.

Just as my actors took a bow, the people running the assembly discovered four non-Shuar in the crowd without proper authorization. Could these be the oil men our scene foretold? Art started to imitate life as, one by one, the assembled Shuar men stood and grabbed their spears. The outsiders panicked and ran, but there was no way they could outrun the Shuar on their own land. The strange men were brought back by force, crying and terrified. Hyper-conscious of my white skin and tall stature, I held well back from where the men were interrogated, watching from the other side of the *espacio cubierto*. A Shuar man had to give the assumed oil prospectors tobacco juice to snort before they would calm down enough to speak. When the commotion had settled, I asked one of my students what happened. "It turned out they were just workers on the road into Makuma," she told me.

The road weighed heavily on everyone's thoughts. In rehearsal when we weren't making explicitly political theater, the scenes my students created centered around the tension they felt between upholding traditional practices and leaving everything behind to make their fortunes in the city. The Shuar spoke of the indigenous groups who lived deeper in the jungle as living "like our grandfathers," and there was a sense that the *colono* cities of the Ecuadorian settlers were the future.

One day, during rehearsal, we heard a scream come from outside the barred windows of our space. We went out to find a local boy, who had been hired to cut the weeds around the building, lying there unmoving. The machete he had been using to chop the jungle back was lying in front of him, next to a downed power line which had been hidden in the tall grass. He was dead. A group of women gathered around the body, wailing, and a growing crowd of men muttered to each other about who to hold responsible. A plane arrived, and the body was loaded on. We stood on the airstrip between the mission and the town, white faces and brown ones alike, and watched the dead boy vanish into the sky.

In my last week of classes, the road arrived in Makuma. Instantly bread was everywhere, fresh in from town, and kids wandered the roads eating sweets they'd never had access to before. A local family took a truck driver hostage—he'd helped a teenaged girl run away to the city, and now no one knew where she was.

But in the midst of all the change, my students, who walked in from communities near and far, found community in each other. They flirted like crazy and laughed shyly whenever someone improvised a romantic scene. It wasn't common to have a space where men and women could interact freely and talk to each other without the watching eyes of the whole community on them. Some days, everyone would bring food and we'd cook together, a three-hour process around an open fire, using large-fronded leaves as oven mitts.

I trained three of my students to continue running the group and making plays after I left, and was proud when one of them reached out months after I'd returned to the US and told me that they'd performed an original piece in the nearest city and been gifted a speaker system for their community. Before I left, the actors I worked with settled on a name for their new group: *Teatro Politico Imiaru. Teatro Politico* just means political theater in Spanish, but *Imiaru* is a Shuar word. It refers to the prophetic hallucinations inspired by ritual practices; an English translation might be "vision of the future." That group has since disbanded, but one of its leaders, Suanua, has started a theater company with the techniques we worked on and actors from her community. Seven years on, I learn from Facebook that they are performing across the country.

Olmedo, one of the kids in my class who was fifteen or sixteen years old when I knew him, reached out to me over Facebook half a decade later. This was a kid who had dropped out of middle school to support his family through farming—in our workshops, Olmedo's Spanish was rusty, and he was hesitant and shy at first in front of the others. A month into classes, he brought me and Victor home to meet his mom, to play soccer with his brothers, and to show off the yucca plot he'd sacrificed everything to tend to. In the years since I'd left, he had completed school and military service, gotten married, and moved to the big city, Quito. On Facebook, he wrote to me:

"I want to get involved more with making theater here. How can I start?"

I had a convert.

# The Story of Us

I'm lost in Macy's. It's 2018 and I'm riding the elevator up and down between the boys' section and home necessities, trying to find my place. Earlier that day I'd thrown my typewriter in the car to drive two hours north of LA, to where they've buried half of a suburban shopping mall underground in the Valley heat. My contact, Camilla, had told me, "Go to handbags and cosmetics on the second floor." That's where the poetry lives today.

It's the weekend before Mother's Day, and in the roped-off event area a striking young black man presides over a legion of pink champagne flutes. Two dour-looking señoras gossip in Spanish while they organize cosmetics, and, opposite them, a fresh-faced young woman has a faraway look next to a heap of pastel macarons capped with a miniature Eiffel Tower.

The first thing Camilla says when I walk up with my typewriter case is, "So, do you need a power outlet?" She asks two more times if I need electricity, as I set up my typewriter on the glass table over a fuzzy pink rug in front of a framed stock photo of roses. Camilla is a short, businesslike woman in bright red lipstick. She proudly shows me the pink Polaroid camera she's brought from home to take pictures of everyone who gets a poem.

Picture and poem both go in a card that says, "The Story of Us," with an ornate flower border.

Only customers who have made a purchase in handbags or cosmetics are allowed to enter our roped-off area. They are led over by their sales reps to recline in a chair for a full facial (I assume—I don't really know what a full facial is) and then take a stool to get their makeup done. From there, they're presented with a pink champagne flute, filled with what I learn, to my disappointment, is just sparkling cider. But after their spa day treatment, they come to talk to me at the typewriter to have a poem written.

Almost everyone I speak with is an immigrant mom, a mix of Asian and Latina women with their American daughters, who range in age from six to forty-six. My poems play across English and Spanish, and I have to pause every few minutes to look up from my typewriter so I can double-check a word or an accent on my iPhone. The American dream of the suburban shopping mall is still alive, it seems, if only for recent immigrants relishing the decadence of American consumerism, bringing their kids to educate them in the native culture of this brave new world.

I write for an adorable six-year-old in a sequined watermelon backpack and her mother, very blond and very Mexican. I read them their poem, as Camilla watches covertly, and the mother dissolves into tears. The water streaks her fresh makeup. I feel guilty for ruining her professionally done face, but also sigh a little in relief—I will be invited back. Camilla asks the mother-daughter pair if she can take a photo, proof for the higher-ups that at least one mom has been genuinely affected by this experience.

I can't help but think of my mom, who didn't even own makeup, waking me up early before she went to work to read to me in hushed tones, nestled on the couch. My Macy's clients were doing the same thing with shopping, in a way, finding an excuse to be close to one another. They always say reading to your kid is a positive, but in my case, it backfired because I was so scared my mom would stop reading to me that I refused to learn to do it myself. How else was I going to know that she still cared?

My reverie is cut short when a woman and her elderly father come up to me. "It'll be your gift for Mom," the woman says to her dad, and asks for a poem for her mother, his wife. The man can only respond when his daughter prompts him. His wife is his caretaker, and from the narrative his daughter puts in his mouth for him to agree with, his wife is a saint. But then I ask the daughter about *her* memories of the woman, and she opens up instantly. "I came to town at the beginning of the year and haven't left," she tells me, exasperated. Her dad's condition is worse than she thought, and her mom is always frustrated and shouting at him. She hadn't meant to stay here, but she did. She had to. She has nothing nice to say about her mother this Mother's Day. She can't find a card that expresses her emotions. This is from her dad, not from her. "Don't put any of this in the poem."

That poem is a hard one to write:

Taking care,
The leaves fall from the trees
But the branches are still
                              beautiful.
We look out our window
       and everything that came before
       try to remember to celebrate
Knowing
       this is what care looks like—
       like frustration,
       like kindness,
       like family
Whose leaves can be green or yellow,
       strong or fallen,
But whose branches carry
The weight of the sky
                         with such grace.

The old man nods and smiles, and I can't tell if he's understood what I said or if this is just his default reaction at this point. His daughter takes the poem and thanks me, her brain already whirring on to the next issue at hand, the next responsibility that she knew would fall to her.

The bartender behind the pink flutes of fake champagne is a "brand ambassador," a beautiful person paid by companies to shill their products at expos and fairs. He says he works in entertainment, another actor, another dreamer, working here at the mall. But then he is sweet and wants a poem for his mom too. He calls her "Maman," she's from France, and now they live on opposite sides of the US and miss each other. He has a shy smile and chooses his words with the care of someone who grew up across languages.

I take a picture of his poem after I write it. Every poem is a potential post, another piece of content I can share online. But it's also a moment of human connection, and the pretty boy bartender crouches down when I read it to him, his eyes closed, a smile starting in the corner of his mouth and growing until it warms his whole face.

For Maman,

Stopping to smell every flower
        as we wend our way across the country
to savor all the history
feast our eyes on museums
        on art, on each other
because we know a country lives
                between us.

Time and distance
are weak enemies. We pay them
                no mind.

We cross the vast expanse—
    we are no strangers to oceans
    and so we are at home everywhere,

Laughing in one another's presence,
    stopping to smell
each leaf and bud
    —we know these are
    the only real things.

The Macy's gig is not atypical of what's become my day-to-day work life, a mix of the saccharine and the sincere. In my flat-cap and vest, I do my best to embody the cliché of the poet for people who would never consider themselves readers of poetry. I occasionally lose out on booking a gig because another poet responds to the email faster or quotes a lower price. We're interchangeable centerpieces, behind our typewriters, just part of the décor. During another gig, a woman at a bar, bemused at my presence behind the typewriter, said to me, "I guess presence is a commodity." For the commodity I provide, I discover, corporate events are common, but it's weddings that are my most consistent market.

It's not every day your average person googles "how to hire a poet" and comes across my website. That day comes somewhere between nine months and three days before they get married.

In Chicago, I write poems for an Irish American couple in the private event space on top of a bar they used to frequent. The minister, a butch, no-nonsense woman, explains the traditional practices that they are bringing to their ceremony and what each means. Their families pass a cord around their hands three times, once for each of them and once for the room, literalizing their bond together. The practice is called "handfasting," I learn. Before the couple place rings on each other's fingers, the rings are passed through the crowd to imbue the spirit of their community in their union. This is not a union of two people, but of two tribes.

The people who ask for a poet at their wedding are rarely fresh-faced young couples but people later in their lives. The theme of self-sufficiency before interdependence ripples through these weddings. Sometimes, it's a second or third wedding. The couple always has money. To get something as unconventional as a typewriter poet, the standards (the flowers, the dinner, the DJ, the bar) have to be taken care of first.

Only then is there space for a poet, an ambassador from the married couple to their community, taking care of their emotional needs on the couple's big day. A few people at any given wedding will get poems for the couple, but most get them for themselves or their own spouses. "Write me a poem about heartbreak," a woman at the Chicago wedding says to me. She had been married twenty-five years. She lost her husband just a few months ago, and here she is, watching another couple tie the knot.

You were mad & I was laughing
& getting things ready
for you to come home

& singing "I found my thrill
    on blueberry hill"
& swearing you heard me
& still hear me
  & after so many years, how
      could you not?

I still hear you
  in barking dogs & the woosh
of fishing lines & in every memory
of the waves off Saint Lucia.

I still hear you & it breaks me
  & I promise you
    I will never stop listening
    I will never stop loving
      the man you were
       & the man you became
       the man who left last July
       & the one I fill every pocket with
like bread,
like prayer.

Somehow it's easier to share intimate aches with a stranger than with the closest friends and family.

"We break the glass to make the world a little less broken," the rabbi at a Jewish wedding near Simi Valley in California says, wrapping a goblet in a cloth sack for the groom to stomp on at the conclusion of another ceremony. I listen to the ministers and rabbis, find the couple's poem in their words to write them in the immediate aftermath of the ceremony before I'm flooded with friends and family.

The rabbi speaks of entering a covenant, the huppa over the couple representing the Garden of Eden before they step out into a new life, the wine they share as a symbol for understanding. The rabbi presents a beautiful scroll of calligraphy in Hebrew and English, the document certifying this union, not for the state, but before a higher power. "We didn't need to get married at this stage of our lives," this couple says, "but we did anyway." As I watch the ceremony, I can't help but think that what I do afterward is a mirror of it, in some ways, making emotions a little more real, a little more fixed, through ritual and documentation. "We didn't need a poem at this stage of our lives, but . . ."

At weddings, I help a community witness itself drawing closer.

"I'm leaving my job," a woman tells me. "I turned fifty this year. I'm hip-deep in life and I want the next half to be intentional. I want to live out my purpose."

"I'm a college senior," says another. "I'm thinking about where I want to live after. Like, where do I want to end up?"

"It's different when it's in service," says a clean-cut medical marijuana grower, who left a job in national security to pursue this line of work. "People tell me they can finally sleep at night." The theme of service comes up, over and over again, people trying to figure out how to fit what they do into how they want to be with other people.

"Write me an ode to being fearless"—this from an older woman with bright red nails and bleached blond hair. Like everyone else in southern California, she's working on a screenplay. Her husband gets a poem too. His theme is "survival," and when I ask him what that means to him all he wants to talk about is music. "I download and listen to a new album every week," he tells me. "Fifty-two new artists a year!"

After a wedding at a winery, the couple reaches out to me to ask me to write a thank-you poem to their photographer, and as I write, I realize that maybe what I do has the same meaning:

Snapshots in time,
  dusty polaroids forgotten
  between the pages of books
      with cracked spines,
corrupted digital files
and when California burns,
    who can say what images
    will escape the ash heap
      of history.
We never wanted fancy shots,
  just a few with eyes
open, a few with good friends,

a few we will not admit
    to sighing over,
we who know the limits
of memory, we aren't kids
    anymore, we don't do it
    for the photo op.
But when the images come back,
we can't help feeling seen
in new ways, can't escape
the gift a camera gives,
a generosity of moments
that won't stop unfolding.

I've been writing poems on the spot since 2012. I've written in three countries and across thirteen states. People are more or less the same, everywhere you go. No matter what the event is, they tell me about their hopes, their sorrows, their spouses, and their dogs. Somehow, before I even start writing, sitting at the typewriter creates permission. Permission for my patrons to sit in their feelings, in their uncertainties. Permission to embrace wherever they may be emotionally and so be able to move forward without fear. I guess sometimes we all just need another person to tell us what we're doing is okay and what we want is allowed. Across age and gender and class and race, across all the lines that divide us from each other, people are shy and sweet when it comes to having a poem written just for them.

Years later, when I run into people I've written for, they recognize me and tell me where in their house they have their poem framed, a daily reminder to themselves of themselves.

Despite my lack of training, people start asking me to teach poetry. At UCLA, college students are almost afraid of the typewriters, raising their hands at the first sign of something unexpected. "You got into UCLA," I scold them lovingly, "figure it out!" They write each other poems about midterms and missing family and romance, earnest and sincere and tender with one another.

In a youth homeless shelter near Venice Beach, a young guy stays after my poetry workshop to talk. He's invented his own font and carries tiny folded books of poetry he's written to sell for a dollar. He's been living on the street for five years now, he tells me, and his memory is going. Writing helps. It's a record that keeps him moored to his past when no home lasts longer than a night.

I tell my students that writing is a way of paying attention. I make them write quickly, without thinking too much. I ask them to hold someone in their heads as they write—their younger self, maybe, or themself on their deathbed, or themself tomorrow. What does that person need to hear? And I ask them to write for each other, to read their work not as a grand literary act with dreams of fame but as an act of intimacy, with an intended audience of one.

I still wince at the idea of teaching, sometimes, thinking about the way poetry seems to ghettoize to underfunded classrooms and lose touch with people as soon as they leave school.

When we teach poetry so often we strip it of its magic, make it all an exercise in form, like some obscure crossword puzzle instead of prayer and rage and comfort and all the human things made language.

I grapple with my anxieties with teaching for ages, before listening to a teacher speak at an open mic and writing for him:

With so many poets
making a living as English teachers
it's tempting to think
that poetry
is only good for kids.

The reality is,
there's just a few of us left
with the quixotic conviction that,
whatever our failings,
maybe the next generation
will be good enough
for poetry.

The great irony is, in the twenty-first century, more people are reading and writing than ever before because of the ubiquity of the internet in the ways we interact with each other, the explosion of social media as a new town square for our digital age. But with an audience of everyone, there's an increasing feeling that no one is listening.

We are isolated. Everything is deliverable, everything is remote—we have no reason to ever leave the house. In removing burdensome tasks, we've inadvertently gutted our spaces of chance encounters, of casual conversation that leads, maybe not to friendship, but to a sense of neighborhood.

It's lonely to see friends more online than in the flesh, and people start to seem more different than the same across the chasm of a digital divide. Work goes this way too, jobs and whole industries popping into and out of existence, human rituals of work constantly perfected by machines and even those machines outdone by newer machines. On social media, my collaborator and friend, poet Linda Ravenswood, talks about the work we do in helping people tell their stories as a "balm against erasure."

The American dream of self-sufficiency through rugged individualism has made our isolation worse. The fastest growing political and religious affiliation is "unaffiliated." Rather than struggle for what it could look like to redefine our institutions, we abandon them without a covenant in place to make sure we can still see each other as members of the same community.

Writing in community after community, I ask myself what it means for poetry to be a service. What are the needs my presence at the typewriter is fulfilling, with a thin veneer of poetry to lend respectability?

This is the best I've come up with: in an age when we witness so much of one another's lives in real time online, we are dying to be seen. In an age when we have the ability, maybe the imperative, to constantly share our stories, we are starving for someone to listen. And in an age when we can reach out to anyone instantly, somehow it's easier to connect with a stranger.

Writing poetry in public works across America because it assures people that they are not alone. Poetry is a little human piece of us, an inmost thought, a hidden desire, a burning question, shared. An assurance in our fractured and atomic age that it's not just us who think and feel how we do.

In 2019, I run an initiative with the City of West Hollywood called Pride Poets, to train queer poets to do typewriter poetry. One of the poets, Natalie Nicole Dressel, tells me afterward how she knew she had enough information from talking to someone to start working on their poem. "I talk to the person until I see myself in them. Then I write that," she says, like it's obvious.

A psychologist I wrote for at a party told me that when we tell each other stories, what we're doing is patterning our brains to be in synch. Neuroimaging suggests that people hearing stories have the same synapses firing as the person telling the story. Sharing memories, sharing stories, is a physical process. Two bodies moving in unison, two brains acting as one brain. Really, the woman at the party says, what's happening in the exchange of a story for a poem is that the person I'm writing for and I are synching brains. Two people with different identities and pasts, finding themselves in each other.

It seems to me that most people just need their stories to be heard. And that *need* is the right word. That we lose something when our stories are not heard. That something not only in us, but in the world, dies.

With every poem I write, I remember that the value of a story doesn't always depend on how many likes or retweets it gets, or how many people it reaches.

Sometimes, just one person hearing a story—is enough.

# Acknowledgments

I always skip forward and read the acknowledgments when I'm three-fourths of the way through a book and hit a complicated paragraph—you ever do that? Part of being a beggar/busker is massive gratitude toward just about everyone. Here's some of it.

For family: My mom, who edits draft after draft for me and still wants to get lunch. My dad, who says things like, "I'm not sure your arguments prove your thesis." I don't have an MFA, but I have these people. For my grandfather, advisor of countless political science dissertations, who advised me "don't wait until your research is finished to write because your research will never be finished." And my grandmother, who drew the horse medicine card for me.

For my team: My editors, Hannah Long, who guided this boat home, and Stephanie Hitchcock, who saw a news story in 2017 and said both, "Have you thought about writing a book?" and "You need an agent to talk to me—I know a guy." My agent, Noah Ballard, who texts me project ideas while on vacation with his girlfriend. Thank you all for taking a chance. I'll never forget sending my first piece to Noah and him saying, "Well, the good news is you can write—neither of us had seen your writing before." Literary fucking miracles.

For the editors who have helped shape these stories: Jessica Reed at *The Guardian*, who helped sculpt and share an early version of "A Poet at the Mall." Jerry Portwood at *Rolling Stone*, who commissioned "After the Fire." And to the editors at the *Mississippi Review* who published "Railroad Writer."

For my support structure: Readers extraordinaire Adrian Rodriguez and Arturo Villarreal, workshopping with the Poetry Salon (Tresha Faye Haefner and Kelly Grace Thomas), mentorship from Charlie Jensen, and co-working space with writers at Writers Blok.

For my colleagues, who keep me dreaming and journeying: Linda Ravenswood, Bobby Gordon, and Nayeli Adorador-Knudsen of Melrose Poetry Bureau (and Craig Knudsen of Knudsen Productions, our manager!). For the Poetry Society of New York, Stephanie Berger and Nicholas Adamski, for scheming up the Poetry Brothel. For Get Lit, Words Ignite and 24th Street Theatre, for inviting this poet from the street into classrooms. For Lady Basco and Beau Sia and all the folks who hold space for other poets to be in community in Los Angeles.

For friends, old and new: Jonathon and Erica and Melody Shekari and Eowyn and their respective families, where they made me feel like I belonged. The Mall of America team, hosts with the most. My train friends, especially Oren. Jeremias for his WhatsApp check-ins and Maria Elena for opening their story to me. My students and partners in Ecuador for their trust, their continued friendship online, and the amazing places they've taken the work we started. And the event planners and wedding photographers who keep me working.

For strangers: Thank you for needing poems. Poems need you.

# About the Author

Brian Sonia-Wallace is the winner of the Amtrak and Mall of America Writer-in-Residence competitions, with additional residencies from the City of Los Angeles, National Parks System, and Dollar Shave Club. His work has been published in *The Guardian* and *Rolling Stone*, and he is the founder of RENT Poet, a poetry-for-hire company featured on NPR's *How I Built This*. Brian was born on a shower curtain in St. Louis, Missouri, and grew up in Los Angeles, where he currently lives with 30+ typewriters.